THE "I LOVE MY AIR FRYER" 5-Ingredient RECIPE BOOK

From *French Toast Sticks* to *Buttermilk-Fried Chicken Thighs*, 175 Quick and Easy Recipes

Robin Fields

Adams Media
New York London Toronto Sydney New Delhi

Adams Media
An Imprint of Simon & Schuster, Inc.
100 Technology Center Drive
Stoughton, Massachusetts 02072

First Adams Media trade paperback edition July 2021

ADAMS MEDIA and colophon are trademarks of Simon & Schuster.

For information about special discounts for bulk purchases, please contact Simon & Schuster Special Sales at 1-866-506-1949 or business@simonandschuster.com.

The Simon & Schuster Speakers Bureau can bring authors to your live event. For more information or to book an event contact the Simon & Schuster Speakers Bureau at 1-866-248-3049 or visit our website at www.simonspeakers.com.

Photographs by James Stefiuk

Manufactured in the United States of America

1 2021

Library of Congress Cataloging-in-Publication Data
Names: Fields, Robin, author.
Title: The "I love my air fryer" 5-ingredient recipe book / Robin Fields.
Description: First Adams Media trade paperback edition. | Stoughton, MA: Adams Media, 2021. | Series: "I love my" series | Includes index.
Identifiers: LCCN 2021003358 | ISBN 9781507216286 (pb) | ISBN 9781507216293 (ebook)
Subjects: LCSH: Hot air frying. | LCGFT: Cookbooks.
Classification: LCC TX689 .F54 2021 | DDC 641.7/7--dc23
LC record available at https://lccn.loc.gov/2021003358

ISBN 978-1-5072-1628-6
ISBN 978-1-5072-1629-3 (ebook)

Always follow safety and commonsense cooking protocols while using kitchen utensils, operating ovens and stoves, and handling uncooked food. If children are assisting in the preparation of any recipe, they should always be supervised by an adult.

Contents

Introduction

Whether you're an air fryer beginner or a veteran, you likely know that this small but mighty appliance has been revolutionizing kitchens everywhere for the past few years with no signs of slowing down. Air fryers continue to rise in popularity not only because they offer reduced cooking times and crispy food without all the oil and fat, but also because they can replace your oven, microwave, deep fryer, and dehydrator. All this saves you time, money, and precious counter space!

Using an air fryer saves time in its own right, and reducing the number of ingredients saves you even more. You don't need a pantry full of hard to find—or hard to pronounce—expensive ingredients in order to make quality meals. The same delicious flavors you love can be achieved with just five main ingredients (or less) and a handful of pantry staples. Developed for busy home cooks of all ages and skills, these recipes use simple preparations, wholesome and delicious ingredients, and best of all, lightning-fast cooking in your amazing air fryer.

In this book, you'll find 175 mouthwatering five-ingredient recipes for every occasion, from game day to Thanksgiving dinner, from breakfasts, lunches, and snacks to filling main courses and delectable desserts—all ready in less time than traditional cooking methods.

Along with delicious recipes and mouthwatering photos, you'll find loads of kitchen hacks and flavoring suggestions to make cooking even more convenient and fitted to your preferences—there are so many ways to cut corners in the kitchen without cutting down on flavor!

Throughout this book you'll learn everything you need to know about using an air fryer, as well as helpful ways to elevate your meals—with only five ingredients—even if you're completely new to cooking. So let's get air frying!

1

Cooking with an Air Fryer

Cooking with an air fryer is as easy as using a microwave. Anybody can do it, and after just a few uses you'll wish you had switched to this genius method of cooking earlier. This chapter will introduce you to air frying options and accessories to maximize your cooking time and get delicious, crispy results. It will also explain how to keep your air fryer clean and offer essentials you'll want to stock up on so that you can whip up a delicious meal with just five ingredients or less any day of the week.

While this chapter will cover the basics of air frying, the first step is reading the manual that came with your air fryer. The recent rise in popularity of the appliance means that you'll find a variety of models with different settings and sizes on the market. A thorough knowledge of how to use your specific air fryer is the key to success and will familiarize you with troubleshooting issues as well as safety functions. Read over the manual and wash all parts with warm, soapy water before first use to help you feel ready to unleash your culinary finesse.

Why Air Frying?

Air frying is increasingly popular because it allows you to quickly and evenly prepare delicious meals with little fat and little effort. Here are just a few of the reasons you'll want to switch to air frying:

- **It replaces other cooking appliances.** You can use the air fryer in place of your oven, microwave, deep fryer, and dehydrator. Using one small device, you can quickly cook perfect dishes for every meal without sacrificing flavor.
- **It cooks faster than traditional cooking methods.** Air frying works by circulating hot air around the cooking chamber. This results in fast and even cooking, using a fraction of the energy of your oven. Most air fryers can be set to a maximum temperature of 400°F, so just about anything you can make in an oven, you can make in an air fryer.
- **It uses little to no cooking oil.** A main selling point of air fryers is that you can achieve beautifully cooked foods using little to no cooking oil. Whether you're following a diet or not, you can probably appreciate lower fat and calorie content. The air fryer helps make that possible.
- **Cleanup is fast.** Any method of cooking will dirty your cooker, but your air fryer's smaller cooking chamber and removable basket make thorough cleanup a breeze!

Choosing an Air Fryer

When choosing an air fryer, the two most important factors to focus on are size and temperature range. Air fryers are usually measured by quart size and range from about 1.2 quarts to 10 or more quarts. Thanks to the number of models available, you can now even find air fryer "ovens"—larger, convection oven–type appliances that you can use to cook multiple racks of food at the same time. This book is based on a four-person air fryer with a 3-quart capacity and 1,425 watts of power. If you're looking to cook meals to feed a family, you might be interested in at least a 5.3-quart fryer that can be used to beautifully roast an entire chicken. If your counter space is limited and you're cooking for only one or two, you can make do with a much smaller air fryer. As for temperature range, some air fryers allow you the ability to dehydrate foods because you can cook them at a very low temperature, say 120°F, for a long period of time. Depending on the functions you need, you'll want to make sure your air fryer has the appropriate cooking capacity and temperature range.

The Functions of an Air Fryer

Most air fryers are equipped with buttons to help you prepare anything from grilling the perfect salmon to roasting an entire chicken or even baking a chocolate cake.

These buttons are programmed to preset times and temperatures based on your specific air fryer. Because of the wide variety of models on the market, all the recipes in this book were created using manual times and temperatures and with an automatic preheat function. If yours doesn't have this function, allow 5 minutes for preheating once you set the desired temperature.

Essential Accessories

Your air fryer's cooking chamber is basically just a large, open space for the hot air to circulate. This is a huge advantage because it gives you the option to incorporate several different accessories into your cooking. These accessories broaden the number of recipes you can make in your air fryer and open up options you never would've thought were possible. Here are some of the common accessories.

- **Metal holder.** This circular rack is used to add a second layer to your cooking surface so you can maximize space and cook multiple things at once. It's particularly helpful when you're cooking meat and vegetables and don't want to wait for one to finish to get started on the other.
- **Skewer rack.** Similar to a metal holder, it has built-in metal skewers that make roasting kebabs a breeze.
- **Ramekins.** Small 4" ramekins are great for making mini cakes and quiches. If they're oven safe, they're safe to use in your air fryer.
- **Cake pans.** You can find specially made cake pans for your air fryer that fit perfectly into the cooking chamber. They also come with a built-in handle so you can easily pull them out when your cakes are done baking.
- **Cupcake pan.** A cupcake pan usually comes with seven mini cups and takes

up the entire chamber of a 5.3-quart air fryer. These versatile cups are perfect for muffins, cupcakes, and even eggs. If you don't want to go this route, you can also use individual silicone baking cups or aluminum cups.

- **Parchment paper.** Any parchment paper will work in the air fryer, but there are some ways to make this step even easier. Specially precut parchment can make cleanup even easier when baking with your air fryer. Additionally, you can find parchment paper with precut holes for easy steaming.
- **Cooking spray.** Although the air fryer cooks with little to no oil, there are some cases in which a little spray is essential. Especially in recipes that involve breading and flour, like fried chicken, spritzing oil on the outside helps you get a brown and crispy exterior for a much tastier end product.

Accessory Removal

Some pans can be more difficult to remove than others because of their size and the depth of the fryer basket. Here are some tools that will allow you to take items out of your appliance safely and easily.

- **Tongs.** These will be helpful when lifting meat in and out of the air fryer. Tongs are also useful for removing cooking pans that don't come with handles.
- **Oven mitts.** Sometimes simple is best. Your food will be very hot when you remove it, so it's great to have these around to protect your hands. Traditional oven mitts or even silicone mitts are great options.

Cleaning Your Air Fryer

Before cleaning it, first ensure that your air fryer is completely cool and unplugged. To clean the air fryer pan you'll need to:

1. Remove the air fryer pan from the base. Fill the pan with hot water and dish soap. Let the pan soak with the frying basket inside for 10 minutes.
2. Clean the basket thoroughly with a sponge or brush.
3. Remove the fryer basket and scrub the underside and outside walls.
4. Clean the air fryer pan with a sponge or brush.
5. Let everything air-dry and return to the air fryer base.

To clean the outside of your air fryer, simply wipe with a damp cloth. Then, be sure all components are in the correct position before beginning your next cooking adventure.

Pantry Staples

Each recipe in this book has five or fewer main ingredients, but also included are some additional kitchen staples to help ensure that the tastes and textures of your meals come out perfect. I've identified six nonperishable pantry staples that you likely already have in your kitchen and that you'll want to have on hand when creating the recipes in this book. These staples are:

- All-purpose flour
- Granulated sugar
- Salt
- Ground black pepper

- Baking powder
- Vanilla extract

These must-haves were chosen for their versatility and frequent use not just in the recipes that follow but also in recipes you may collect online, at family gatherings and parties, and more. In each recipe in this book, you'll find a list of which of these staples you'll also need, so be sure to stock up on anything you may be running low on beforehand.

With this final information in hand, you are truly ready to get cooking. Throughout the following chapters you'll find plenty of delicious, five-ingredient recipes to suit all tastes. Use these recipes as your guide, but always feel free to season intuitively and customize dishes to your liking—just be aware that doing so will change the provided nutritional information.

2

Breakfast

Mornings are usually the busiest part of everyone's day. In the midst of all of the chaos, it seems like there's never enough time to get yourself and everyone else ready while still getting a filling breakfast on the table that you actually want to eat. While it can be easy to just swing by the drive-through, there's something satisfying about feeding your family nourishing, homemade meals with ingredients you can actually pronounce. This chapter is here to give you just that. Pretty soon, your air fryer will be your morning's new favorite companion. From French Toast Sticks to Crispy Bacon, this chapter covers tasty breakfast favorites that will get your day started right!

Easy Egg Bites

For a grab-and-go breakfast that's sure to please, it doesn't get much easier than egg bites. Not only are these delicious bites quick to make and filling, they're also highly customizable to any flavor profile you're craving, from southwest style to Italian herb.

Pantry Staples: salt, ground black pepper
Hands-On Time: 5 minutes
Cook Time: 9 minutes

Serves 2

- 2 large eggs
- ¼ cup full-fat cottage cheese
- ¼ cup shredded sharp Cheddar cheese
- ¼ teaspoon salt
- ⅛ teaspoon ground black pepper
- 6 tablespoons diced cooked ham

1. Preheat the air fryer to 300°F. Spray six silicone muffin cups with cooking spray.
2. In a blender, place eggs, cottage cheese, Cheddar, salt, and pepper. Pulse five times until smooth and frothy.
3. Place 1 tablespoon ham in the bottom of each prepared baking cup, then divide egg mixture among cups.
4. Place in the air fryer basket and cook 9 minutes until egg bites are firm in the center. Carefully remove cups from air fryer basket and cool 3 minutes before serving. Serve warm.

PER SERVING

CALORIES: 210 | **FAT:** 12g | **PROTEIN:** 21g | **SODIUM:** 1,080mg | **FIBER:** 0g | **CARBOHYDRATES:** 2g | **SUGAR:** 1g

Breakfast Bake

Whether you're cooking ahead for the week or need a last-minute breakfast idea, this dish is the perfect springboard for your day. This meal couldn't be easier and can even be prepared the night before to save more time. Feel free to swap the breakfast sausage for your favorite protein, such as cooked bacon or ham.

Pantry Staples: salt, ground black pepper
Hands-On Time: 5 minutes
Cook Time: 15 minutes

Serves 4

- 6 large eggs
- 2 tablespoons heavy cream
- ½ teaspoon salt
- ¼ teaspoon ground black pepper
- ⅓ pound ground pork breakfast sausage, cooked and drained
- ½ cup shredded Cheddar cheese

1. Preheat the air fryer to 320°F. Spray a 6" round cake pan with cooking spray.
2. In a large bowl, whisk eggs, cream, salt, and pepper until fully combined.
3. Arrange cooked sausage in the bottom of prepared pan. Pour egg mixture into pan on top of sausage. Sprinkle Cheddar on top.
4. Place in the air fryer basket and cook 15 minutes until the top begins to brown and the center is set. Let cool 5 minutes before serving. Serve warm.

PER SERVING

CALORIES: 340 | **FAT:** 29g | **PROTEIN:** 18g | **SODIUM:** 880mg | **FIBER:** 0g | **CARBOHYDRATES:** 1g | **SUGAR:** 1g

CUSTOMIZE IT

Try adding chopped vegetables such as bell peppers, sliced mushrooms, or diced onions to make this dish your own. If you are a meat lover, try adding additional sausage or even crumbled bacon.

Egg White Frittata

If you're looking for a lighter option without sacrificing flavor, egg whites are a great stand-in for regular eggs. This light and healthy breakfast is still plenty filling, thanks in part to the delicious vegetables that round out the dish.

Pantry Staples: salt
Hands-On Time: 5 minutes
Cook Time: 8 minutes

Serves 2

2 cups liquid egg whites
½ cup chopped fresh spinach
¼ cup chopped Roma tomato
½ teaspoon salt
¼ cup chopped white onion

1. Preheat the air fryer to 320°F. Spray a 6" round baking dish with cooking spray.
2. In a large bowl, whisk egg whites until frothy. Mix in spinach, tomato, salt, and onion. Stir until combined.
3. Pour egg mixture into prepared dish.
4. Place in the air fryer basket and cook 8 minutes until the center is set. Serve warm.

PER SERVING

CALORIES: 150 | **FAT:** 0g | **PROTEIN:** 27g | **SODIUM:** 990mg | **FIBER:** 1g | **CARBOHYDRATES:** 8g | **SUGAR:** 1g

Chocolate Chip Scones

Scones may seem intimidating, but as long as you keep the butter cold, you'll soon be enjoying a flaky, delicious breakfast treat. The air fryer gets the edges even crispier and more brown in less time than the oven does. This recipe uses buttermilk for a flavorful tang, but you can swap it out for an equal amount of regular milk if that's what you have on hand.

Pantry Staples: all-purpose flour, baking powder
Hands-On Time: 15 minutes
Cook Time: 15 minutes per batch

Serves 8

½ cup cold salted butter, divided
2 cups all-purpose flour
½ cup brown sugar
½ teaspoon baking powder
1 large egg
¾ cup buttermilk
½ cup semisweet chocolate chips

1. Preheat the air fryer to 320°F. Cut parchment paper to fit the air fryer basket.
2. Chill 6 tablespoons butter in the freezer 10 minutes. In a small microwave-safe bowl, microwave remaining 2 tablespoons butter 30 seconds until melted, and set aside.
3. In a large bowl, mix flour, brown sugar, and baking powder.
4. Remove butter from freezer and grate into bowl. Use a wooden spoon to evenly distribute.
5. Add egg and buttermilk and stir gently until a soft, sticky dough forms. Gently fold in chocolate chips.
6. Turn dough out onto a lightly floured surface. Fold a couple of times and gently form into a 6" round. Cut into eight triangles.
7. Place scones on parchment in the air fryer basket, leaving at least 2" space between each, working in batches as necessary.
8. Brush each scone with melted butter. Cook 15 minutes until scones are dark golden brown and crispy on the edges, and a toothpick inserted into the center comes out clean. Serve warm.

PER SERVING (SERVING SIZE: 1 SCONE)

CALORIES: 330 | **FAT:** 16g | **PROTEIN:** 5g | **SODIUM:** 35mg | **FIBER:** 2g | **CARBOHYDRATES:** 44g | **SUGAR:** 19g

Blueberry Scones

Skip the coffee shop pastry on your morning commute. These blueberry scones are delicious and so easy to make in your air fryer. They're the perfect mix of flaky, buttery, and sweet. If you only have frozen blueberries, allow them to fully thaw before using them to avoid excess water in the batter.

Pantry Staples: all-purpose flour, granulated sugar, baking powder
Hands-On Time: 15 minutes
Cook Time: 15 minutes per batch

Serves 8

½ cup cold salted butter, divided
2 cups all-purpose flour
½ cup granulated sugar
1 teaspoon baking powder
1 large egg
½ cup whole milk
½ cup fresh blueberries

1. Chill 6 tablespoons butter in the freezer 10 minutes. In a small microwave-safe bowl, microwave remaining 2 tablespoons butter 30 seconds until melted.
2. Preheat the air fryer to 320°F. Cut parchment paper to fit the air fryer basket.
3. In a large bowl, mix flour, sugar, and baking powder
4. Add egg and milk and stir until a sticky dough forms.
5. Remove butter from freezer and grate into bowl. Fold grated butter into dough until just combined.
6. Fold in blueberries. Turn dough onto a lightly floured surface. Sprinkle dough with flour and fold a couple of times, then gently form into a 6" round. Cut into eight triangles.
7. Place scones on parchment in the air fryer basket, leaving at least 2" of space between each, working in batches as necessary.
8. Brush each scone with melted butter and cook 15 minutes until scones are dark golden brown and crispy on the edges, and a toothpick inserted into the center comes out clean. Serve warm.

PER SERVING (SERVING SIZE: 1 SCONE)

CALORIES: 280 | **FAT:** 13g | **PROTEIN:** 4g | **SODIUM:** 105mg | **FIBER:** 1g | **CARBOHYDRATES:** 39g | **SUGAR:** 14g

LEMON GLAZE

To add a tangy pop of flavor, add 1 tablespoon lemon zest to this dough before baking. Then make a lemon glaze by whisking together ⅓ cup confectioners' sugar, 2 teaspoons heavy cream, and 1 teaspoon lemon juice in a small bowl. Drizzle over the scones after cooling.

Banana Baked Oatmeal

After just a few minutes of prep time you'll be enjoying a bowl of oatmeal in a fraction of the time it takes to cook on the stove. The edges get brown and crispy while the creamy center gives it the perfect baked oatmeal texture.

Pantry Staples: vanilla extract, salt
Hands-On Time: 5 minutes
Cook Time: 10 minutes

Serves 2

1 cup quick-cooking oats
1 cup whole milk
2 tablespoons unsalted butter, melted
1 medium banana, peeled and mashed
2 tablespoons brown sugar
½ teaspoon vanilla extract
½ teaspoon salt

CUSTOMIZE IT

Not a fan of bananas? Feel free to omit them and add an extra ½ teaspoon of sweetener such as sugar or maple syrup. You can also try mixing in fresh blueberries or pecans or adding a sprinkle of cinnamon.

1. Preheat the air fryer to 360°F.
2. In a 6" round pan, add oats. Pour in milk and butter.
3. In a medium bowl, mix banana, brown sugar, vanilla, and salt until combined. Add to pan and mix until well combined.
4. Place in the air fryer and cook 10 minutes until the top is brown and oats feel firm to the touch. Serve warm.

PER SERVING

CALORIES: 470 | **FAT:** 19g | **PROTEIN:** 12g | **SODIUM:** 640mg | **FIBER:** 7g | **CARBOHYDRATES:** 63g | **SUGAR:** 29g

Blueberry Muffins

You can make these ahead, freeze them, and reheat in your air fryer anytime you're ready for a yummy breakfast treat. To reheat, place in the air fryer basket at 120°F for 3 minutes. Store leftovers in an airtight container in the refrigerator up to 3 days or in an airtight freezer-safe bag in the freezer up to 3 months.

Pantry Staples: all-purpose flour, granulated sugar, baking powder
Hands-On Time: 5 minutes
Cook Time: 15 minutes per batch

Serves 12

1 cup all-purpose flour
½ cup granulated sugar
1 teaspoon baking powder
¼ cup salted butter, melted
1 large egg
½ cup whole milk
1 cup fresh blueberries

1. Preheat the air fryer to 300°F.
2. In a large bowl, whisk together flour, sugar, and baking powder.
3. Add butter, egg, and milk to dry mixture. Stir until well combined.
4. Gently fold in blueberries. Divide batter evenly among twelve silicone or aluminum muffin cups, filling cups about halfway full.
5. Place cups in the air fryer basket, working in batches as necessary. Cook 15 minutes until muffins are brown at the edges and a toothpick inserted in the center comes out clean. Serve warm.

PER SERVING (SERVING SIZE: 1 MUFFIN)

CALORIES: 120 | **FAT:** 4.5g | **PROTEIN:** 2g | **SODIUM:** 10mg | **FIBER:** 1g | **CARBOHYDRATES:** 19g | **SUGAR:** 10g

Flaky Cinnamon Rolls

This recipe brings a fun twist to classic cinnamon rolls. Puff pastry provides a wonderfully light and flaky texture in every single bite. The cinnamon and sugar make these rolls extra gooey and caramelized on the outside. Try adding a few tablespoons of finely chopped pecans for an extra crunch.

Pantry Staples: granulated sugar
Hands-On Time: 10 minutes
Cook Time: 12 minutes per batch

Serves 8

- **1 sheet frozen puff pastry, thawed**
- **6 tablespoons unsalted butter, melted**
- **¾ cup granulated sugar**
- **2 tablespoons ground cinnamon**
- **½ cup confectioners' sugar**
- **2 tablespoons heavy cream**

1. Preheat the air fryer to 320°F. Cut parchment paper to fit the air fryer basket.
2. Unroll puff pastry into a large rectangle. Brush with butter, then evenly sprinkle sugar and cinnamon around dough, coating as evenly as possible.
3. Starting at one of the long sides, roll dough into a log, then use a little water on your fingers to seal the edge.
4. Slice dough into eight rounds. Place on parchment in the air fryer basket, working in batches as necessary, and cook 12 minutes until golden brown and flaky. Let cool 5 minutes.
5. In a small bowl, whisk confectioners' sugar and cream together until smooth. Drizzle over cinnamon rolls and serve.

PER SERVING (SERVING SIZE: 1 ROLL)

CALORIES: 220 | **FAT:** 11g | **PROTEIN:** 1g | **SODIUM:** 30mg | **FIBER:** 1g | **CARBOHYDRATES:** 30g | **SUGAR:** 26g

Strawberry Pastry

You won't need a toaster for these delicious homemade pastries. Sweet, flaky, and bursting with strawberry flavor, this breakfast will remind you of your childhood favorite from the frozen food aisle. This recipe uses premade crust to save time, but feel free to use a homemade crust if you prefer.

Pantry Staples: vanilla extract
Hands-On Time: 10 minutes
Cook Time: 15 minutes per batch

Serves 8

1 (15-ounce) package refrigerated piecrust
1 cup strawberry jam
1 large egg, whisked
½ cup confectioners' sugar
2 tablespoons whole milk
½ teaspoon vanilla extract

CHANGE IT UP

If you're not a fan of strawberries, switch out the jam in this recipe for your favorite fruit flavor or even a spoonful of Nutella.

1. Preheat the air fryer to 320°F. Cut parchment paper to fit the air fryer basket.
2. On a lightly floured surface, lay piecrusts out flat. Cut each piecrust round into six 4" × 3" rectangles, reserving excess dough.
3. Form remaining dough into a ball, then roll out and cut four additional 4" × 3" rectangles, bringing the total to sixteen.
4. For each pastry, spread 2 tablespoons jam on a pastry rectangle, leaving a 1" border around the edges. Top with a second pastry rectangle and use a fork to gently press all four edges together. Repeat with remaining jam and pastry.
5. Brush tops of each pastry with egg and cut an *X* in the center of each to prevent excess steam from building up.
6. Place pastries on parchment in the air fryer basket, working in batches as necessary. Cook 12 minutes, then carefully flip and cook an additional 3 minutes until each side is golden brown. Let cool 10 minutes.
7. In a small bowl, whisk confectioners' sugar, milk, and vanilla. Brush each pastry with glaze, then place in the refrigerator 5 minutes to set before serving.

PER SERVING (SERVING SIZE: 1 PASTRY)

CALORIES: 380 | **FAT:** 14g | **PROTEIN:** 2g | **SODIUM:** 220mg | **FIBER:** 0g | **CARBOHYDRATES:** 61g | **SUGAR:** 32g

Bagels

This recipe lets you enjoy a fresh bagel in a fraction of the time they usually take to make. Chewy and warm with a golden glistening crust, these Bagels are the perfect morning staple. If you're a fan of everything bagel seasoning or toasted sesame seeds, simply sprinkle them over the top before baking for added flavor and crunch.

Pantry Staples: granulated sugar
Hands-On Time: 10 minutes
Cook Time: 10 minutes

Serves 4

1 cup self-rising flour
1 cup plain full-fat Greek yogurt
2 tablespoons granulated sugar
1 large egg, whisked

MAKE IT A SANDWICH

These bagels will make a filling and tasty sandwich. Simply let cool, then slice in half. Place in the air fryer at 400°F for 5 minutes to toast, or pop into your toaster. Add bacon or sausage and a fried egg, and you're ready to start your day.

1. Preheat the air fryer to 320°F.
2. In a large bowl, mix flour, yogurt, and sugar together until a ball of dough forms.
3. Turn dough out onto a lightly floured surface. Knead dough for 3 minutes, then form into a smooth ball. Cut dough into four sections. Roll each piece into an 8" rope, then shape into a circular bagel shape. Brush top and bottom of each bagel with egg.
4. Place in the air fryer basket and cook 10 minutes, turning halfway through cooking time to ensure even browning. Let cool 5 minutes before serving.

PER SERVING

CALORIES: 220 | **FAT:** 5g | **PROTEIN:** 11g | **SODIUM:** 430mg | **FIBER:** 1g | **CARBOHYDRATES:** 32g | **SUGAR:** 9g

Hard-"Boiled" Eggs

You can hard-"boil" whole eggs right in your air fryer basket. Just pop them in and let the air fryer work its magic. Don't worry if your eggs come out with brown spots on the eggshells; this can be caused by extra condensation or leftover grease splatter.

Pantry Staples: none
Hands-On Time: 2 minutes
Cook Time: 15 minutes

Serves 6

6 large eggs

1 Preheat the air fryer to 280°F.

2 Place eggs in the air fryer basket and cook 15 minutes. Store cooked eggs in the refrigerator until ready to use, or peel and serve warm.

PER SERVING

CALORIES: 70 | **FAT:** 5g | **PROTEIN:** 6g | **SODIUM:** 70mg | **FIBER:** 0g | **CARBOHYDRATES:** 0g | **SUGAR:** 0g

Crispy Bacon

Get ready for a bacon-cooking technique that you can pretty much set and forget. Ten minutes is all that stands between you and deliciously crispy air fried bacon.

Pantry Staples: none
Hands-On Time: 5 minutes
Cook Time: 10 minutes

Serves 4

8 slices bacon

1 Preheat the air fryer to 400°F.

2 Lay bacon in the air fryer basket in a single layer.

3 Cook 10 minutes, turning halfway through cooking time. Remove from the air fryer and place on a paper towel to absorb excess grease. Serve warm.

PER SERVING

CALORIES: 230 | **FAT:** 22g | **PROTEIN:** 7g | **SODIUM:** 370mg | **FIBER:** 0g | **CARBOHYDRATES:** 1g | **SUGAR:** 1g

Roasted Golden Mini Potatoes

These potatoes are buttery smooth on the inside and crispy on the edges, which makes them perfect to enjoy alone or even with a sauce like sausage gravy.

Pantry Staples: salt, ground black pepper
Hands-On Time: 5 minutes
Cook Time: 22 minutes

Serves 4

6 cups water
1 pound baby Dutch yellow potatoes, quartered
2 tablespoons olive oil
½ teaspoon garlic powder
¾ teaspoon seasoned salt
¼ teaspoon salt
⅛ teaspoon ground black pepper

1 In a medium saucepan over medium-high heat bring water to a boil. Add potatoes and boil 10 minutes until fork-tender, then drain and gently pat dry.
2 Preheat the air fryer to 400°F.
3 Drizzle oil over potatoes, then sprinkle with garlic powder, seasoned salt, salt, and pepper.
4 Place potatoes in the air fryer basket and cook 12 minutes, shaking the basket three times during cooking. Potatoes will be done when golden brown and edges are crisp. Serve warm.

PER SERVING

CALORIES: 150 | **FAT:** 7g | **PROTEIN:** 2g | **SODIUM:** 440mg | **FIBER:** 2g | **CARBOHYDRATES:** 22g | **SUGAR:** 0g

Sweet and Spicy Breakfast Sausage

These sausages caramelize on the edges and are sweet with just a hint of spicy. They are perfect to make ahead of time too. To reheat, cook 5 minutes in the air fryer at 120°F.

Pantry Staples: salt, ground black pepper
Hands-On Time: 5 minutes
Cook Time: 10 minutes

Serves 6

1 pound 84% lean ground pork
2 tablespoons brown sugar
1 teaspoon salt
½ teaspoon ground black pepper
½ teaspoon garlic powder
½ teaspoon dried fennel
½ teaspoon crushed red pepper flakes

1 Preheat the air fryer to 400°F.
2 In a large bowl, mix all ingredients until well combined. Divide mixture into eight portions and form into patties.
3 Spritz patties with cooking spray and place in the air fryer basket. Cook 10 minutes until patties are brown and internal temperature reaches at least 145°F. Serve warm.

PER SERVING

CALORIES: 190 | **FAT:** 12g | **PROTEIN:** 14g | **SODIUM:** 440mg | **FIBER:** 0g | **CARBOHYDRATES:** 6g | **SUGAR:** 5g

French Toast Sticks

This is one of the easiest ways to recreate a classic breakfast favorite without ever picking up a skillet. In just minutes, you'll have sweet, delicious, dippable sticks for an easy, family-friendly breakfast.

Pantry Staples: granulated sugar
Hands-On Time: 5 minutes
Cook Time: 8 minutes

Serves 4

4 slices Texas toast, or other thick-sliced bread
2 large eggs
¼ cup heavy cream
4 tablespoons salted butter, melted
½ cup granulated sugar
1½ tablespoons ground cinnamon

1. Preheat the air fryer to 350°F. Cut parchment paper to fit the air fryer basket.
2. Slice each piece of bread into four even sticks.
3. In a medium bowl, whisk together eggs and cream. Dip each bread stick into mixture and place on parchment in the air fryer basket.
4. Cook 5 minutes, then carefully turn over and cook an additional 3 minutes until golden brown on both sides.
5. Drizzle sticks with butter and toss to ensure they're covered on all sides.
6. In a medium bowl, mix sugar and cinnamon. Dip both sides of each stick into the mixture and shake off excess. Serve warm.

PER SERVING (SERVING SIZE: 4 STICKS)

CALORIES: 440 | **FAT:** 26g | **PROTEIN:** 7g | **SODIUM:** 400mg | **FIBER:** 1g | **CARBOHYDRATES:** 47g | **SUGAR:** 20g

Banana-Nut Muffins

These muffins are fluffy, sweet, and perfect for any breakfast or snack. You don't need a long list of ingredients to get the flavor you love. These muffins keep well in the refrigerator up to 4 days but can also be individually wrapped in plastic and frozen in an airtight storage bag for up to 2 months.

Pantry Staples: all-purpose flour, granulated sugar, baking powder
Hands-On Time: 5 minutes
Cook Time: 15 minutes per batch

Serves 12

1½ cups all-purpose flour
½ cup granulated sugar
1 teaspoon baking powder
½ cup salted butter, melted
1 large egg
2 medium bananas, peeled and mashed
½ cup chopped pecans

1. Preheat the air fryer to 300°F.
2. In a large bowl, whisk together flour, sugar, and baking powder.
3. Add butter, egg, and bananas to dry mixture. Stir until well combined. Batter will be thick.
4. Gently fold in pecans. Divide batter evenly among twelve silicone or aluminum muffin cups, filling cups about halfway full.
5. Place cups in the air fryer basket, working in batches as necessary. Cook 15 minutes until muffin edges are brown and a toothpick inserted into the center comes out clean. Let cool 5 minutes before serving.

PER SERVING (SERVING SIZE: 1 MUFFIN)

CALORIES: 210 | **FAT:** 11g | **PROTEIN:** 3g | **SODIUM:** 65mg | **FIBER:** 1g | **CARBOHYDRATES:** 26g | **SUGAR:** 11g

Hash Browns

Dark golden brown tops and edges make these Hash Browns delicious and perfect for any meal. They're quick enough to make in the morning but also make an excellent side dish. This ultra-crispy meal addition can be enjoyed with mix-ins like chopped peppers and onions for even more flavor.

Pantry Staples: salt
Hands-On Time: 5 minutes
Cook Time: 30 minutes

Serves 2

- 2 large russet potatoes, peeled
- 2 cups cold water
- 1 tablespoon olive oil
- ½ teaspoon salt

1. Grate potatoes into a bowl filled with cold water. Let soak 10 minutes. Drain into a colander, then press into paper towels to remove excess moisture.
2. Dry the bowl and return potatoes to it. Toss with oil and salt.
3. Preheat the air fryer to 375°F. Spray a 6" round cake pan with cooking spray.
4. Pour potatoes into prepared pan, pressing them down.
5. Cook 20 minutes until brown and crispy. Serve warm.

PER SERVING

CALORIES: 230 | **FAT:** 7g | **PROTEIN:** 5g | **SODIUM:** 590mg | **FIBER:** 3g | **CARBOHYDRATES:** 40g | **SUGAR:** 2g

Scotch Eggs

Having Scotch Eggs for breakfast gives you the protein boost you need to help power through your day. These hard-cooked eggs are covered in juicy breakfast sausage and bread crumbs for the perfect complete meal. You can even hard-cook your eggs without water, right in your air fryer. Check out the Hard-"Boiled" Eggs recipe in this chapter.

Pantry Staples: all-purpose flour
Hands-On Time: 10 minutes
Cook Time: 15 minutes

Serves 6

- **1 pound ground pork breakfast sausage**
- **6 large hard-boiled eggs, peeled**
- **1 cup all-purpose flour**
- **2 large eggs, beaten**
- **2 cups plain bread crumbs**

1. Preheat the air fryer to 375°F.
2. Separate sausage into six equal amounts and flatten into patties.
3. Form sausage patties around hard-boiled eggs, completely enclosing them.
4. In three separate small bowls, place flour, eggs, and bread crumbs.
5. Roll each sausage-covered egg first in flour, then egg, and finally bread crumbs. Place rolled eggs in the air fryer basket and spritz them with cooking spray.
6. Cook 15 minutes, turning halfway through cooking time and spraying any dry spots with additional cooking spray. Serve warm.

PER SERVING

CALORIES: 610 | **FAT:** 37g | **PROTEIN:** 25g | **SODIUM:** 1,130mg | **FIBER:** 1g | **CARBOHYDRATES:** 42g | **SUGAR:** 2g

PERFECT DIPPING SAUCE

The perfect dipping sauce makes this whole meal. In a small bowl, whisk together ⅓ cup mayonnaise and 1 tablespoon sriracha to make a creamy dip with a spicy kick!

Maple-Bacon Doughnuts

Maple-Bacon Doughnuts are the perfect sweet and savory way to get your morning started right. It's easy to convert refrigerated biscuit dough into perfect doughnuts right in your air fryer. You can learn more about how to get perfectly cooked air fryer bacon in the Crispy Bacon recipe in this chapter.

Pantry Staples: none
Hands-On Time: 5 minutes
Cook Time: 5 minutes

Serves 8

- 1 (16.3-ounce) can refrigerated biscuit dough, separated
- 1 cup confectioners' sugar
- ¼ cup heavy cream
- 1 teaspoon maple extract
- 6 slices bacon, cooked and crumbled

1. Preheat the air fryer to 350°F.
2. Place biscuits in the air fryer basket and cook 5 minutes, turning halfway through cooking time, until golden brown. Let cool 5 minutes.
3. In a medium bowl, whisk together confectioners' sugar, cream, and maple extract until smooth.
4. Dip top of each doughnut into glaze and set aside to set for 5 minutes. Top with crumbled bacon and serve immediately.

PER SERVING

CALORIES: 240 | **FAT:** 6g | **PROTEIN:** 6g | **SODIUM:** 570mg | **FIBER:** 0g | **CARBOHYDRATES:** 42g | **SUGAR:** 18g

Egg in a Hole

If you're short on time in the morning, this might just become a favorite go-to breakfast. It's easy, convenient, and portable. While this dish is traditionally prepared in a skillet, you can make this meal in 15 minutes in the air fryer with minimal supervision.

Pantry Staples: salt, ground black pepper
Hands-On Time: 5 minutes
Cook Time: 10 minutes per batch

Serves 4

- **4 slices white sandwich bread**
- **4 large eggs**
- **½ teaspoon salt**
- **¼ teaspoon ground black pepper**

1. Preheat the air fryer to 350°F. Spray a 6" round cake pan with cooking spray.
2. Place as many pieces of bread as will fit in one layer in prepared pan, working in batches as necessary.
3. Using a small cup or cookie cutter, cut a circle out of the center of each bread slice. Crack an egg directly into each cutout and sprinkle eggs with salt and pepper.
4. Cook 5 minutes, then carefully turn and cook an additional 5 minutes or less, depending on your preference. Serve warm.

PER SERVING

CALORIES: 140 | **FAT:** 6g | **PROTEIN:** 8g | **SODIUM:** 490mg | **FIBER:** 0g | **CARBOHYDRATES:** 12g | **SUGAR:** 2g

Breakfast Quiche

This meal uses a premade piecrust to cut down on time and effort in the kitchen. In less than 30 minutes you can enjoy a creamy and fluffy quiche made right in the air fryer. To make this meal your own, add your favorite chopped mix-ins such as caramelized onions, sautéed vegetables, or extra meat.

Pantry Staples: salt, ground black pepper
Hands-On Time: 10 minutes
Cook Time: 18 minutes

Serves 4

- **1 (9") refrigerated piecrust**
- **2 large eggs**
- **¼ cup heavy cream**
- **½ teaspoon salt**
- **¼ teaspoon ground black pepper**
- **½ cup shredded Cheddar cheese**
- **2 slices bacon, cooked and crumbled**

1. Preheat the air fryer to 325°F. Spray a 6" pie pan with cooking spray. Trim piecrust to fit the pan.
2. In a medium bowl, whisk together eggs, cream, salt, and pepper. Stir in Cheddar and bacon.
3. Pour egg mixture into crust and cook 18 minutes until firm, brown, and a knife inserted into the center comes out clean. Serve warm.

PER SERVING

CALORIES: 350 | **FAT:** 24g | **PROTEIN:** 10g | **SODIUM:** 660mg | **FIBER:** 0g | **CARBOHYDRATES:** 23g | **SUGAR:** 2g

Cream Cheese Danish

This bakery-style danish is perfect for all pastry lovers. Each bite is full of flaky, buttery goodness. The center is sweet and creamy, making this perfect for breakfast or dessert. Feel free to add a teaspoon of your favorite jam to the center before cooking.

Pantry Staples: vanilla extract
Hands-On Time: 5 minutes
Cook Time: 10 minutes

Serves 4

- **1 sheet frozen puff pastry dough, thawed**
- **1 large egg, beaten**
- **4 ounces full-fat cream cheese, softened**
- **¼ cup confectioners' sugar**
- **1 teaspoon vanilla extract**
- **½ teaspoon lemon juice**

1. Preheat the air fryer to 320°F.
2. Unfold puff pastry and cut into four equal squares. For each pastry, fold all four corners partway to the center, leaving a 1" square in the center.
3. Brush egg evenly over folded puff pastry.
4. In a medium bowl, mix cream cheese, confectioners' sugar, vanilla, and lemon juice. Scoop 2 tablespoons of mixture into the center of each pastry square.
5. Place danishes directly in the air fryer basket and cook 10 minutes until puffy and golden brown. Cool 5 minutes before serving.

PER SERVING

CALORIES: 190 | **FAT:** 14g | **PROTEIN:** 4g | **SODIUM:** 160mg | **FIBER:** 0g | **CARBOHYDRATES:** 13g | **SUGAR:** 9g

Chocolate-Hazelnut Bear Claws

Mornings seem easier when you have a chocolate pastry to look forward to. These are filled with a rich, creamy spread that makes every bite delectable.

Pantry Staples: none
Hands-On Time: 5 minutes
Cook Time: 10 minutes

Serves 4

- **1 sheet frozen puff pastry dough, thawed**
- **1 large egg, beaten**
- **½ cup chocolate-hazelnut spread**
- **1 tablespoon confectioners' sugar**
- **1 tablespoon sliced almonds**

1. Preheat the air fryer to 320°F.
2. Unfold puff pastry and cut into four equal squares.
3. Brush egg evenly over puff pastry.
4. To make each bear claw, spread 2 tablespoons chocolate-hazelnut spread over a pastry square. Fold square horizontally to form a triangle and cut four evenly spaced slits about halfway through the top of folded square. Repeat with remaining spread and pastry squares.
5. Sprinkle confectioners' sugar and almonds over bear claws and place directly in the air fryer basket. Cook 10 minutes until puffy and golden brown. Serve warm.

PER SERVING

CALORIES: 280 | **FAT:** 16g | **PROTEIN:** 5g | **SODIUM:** 85mg | **FIBER:** 0g | **CARBOHYDRATES:** 29g | **SUGAR:** 22g

3

Appetizers and Snacks

From game day parties to before-dinner treats, appetizers and snacks are the perfect little bites to help everyone connect over something tasty or bridge the gap between meals. Sometimes the prep work to get your impressive table spreads together can be draining, but the good news is you can create delicious, restaurant-quality appetizers right in your air fryer in no time. There's no need to fuss with rare, expensive ingredients or overly complicated steps. From football favorites like Buffalo Chicken Wings to kid-friendly classics like Ham and Cheese Sliders, this chapter has you covered and ready for snacking bliss!

Potato Chips

When you're looking for something satisfying to munch on, Potato Chips are a must-have. These made-from-scratch chips come together quickly and you'll feel great eating this snack knowing it's made with simple ingredients.

Pantry Staples: salt
Hands-On Time: 10 minutes
Cook Time: 50 minutes

Serves 4

2 large russet potatoes
½ teaspoon salt

CUSTOMIZE IT

These chips taste great with all your favorite chip seasonings. After cooking, place the chips in a large bowl and toss with 2 teaspoons dry ranch seasoning, your favorite dry barbecue mix, or even spritz with a little vinegar.

1. Cut 1" off top and bottom of each potato. Using a mandoline, thinly slice each potato.
2. Place potato slices in a bowl of cold water 30 minutes.
3. Preheat the air fryer to 300°F.
4. Drain and pat potato slices dry, then spritz with cooking spray. Place in the air fryer basket and cook 15 minutes. Shake the basket twice during cooking time.
5. Increase temperature to 400°F and cook an additional 5 minutes until chips are light brown. Sprinkle with salt.
6. Place on a paper towel to cool 5 minutes.

PER SERVING

CALORIES: 80 | **FAT:** 0g | **PROTEIN:** 2g | **SODIUM:** 290mg | **FIBER:** 2g | **CARBOHYDRATES:** 20g | **SUGAR:** 1g

Onion Rings

Crispy, golden, and perfect as a side dish or on top of a burger, this recipe is very versatile. Whether you prefer to dip them or enjoy them alone and let the flavor speak for itself, these Onion Rings will become your new go-to recipe.

Pantry Staples: all-purpose flour
Hands-On Time: 15 minutes
Cook Time: 12 minutes

Serves 4

1 cup all-purpose flour
1 tablespoon seasoned salt
1 cup whole milk
1 large egg
1 cup panko bread crumbs
1 large Vidalia onion, peeled and sliced into ¼"-thick rings

1. Preheat the air fryer to 350°F.
2. In a large bowl, whisk together flour and seasoned salt.
3. In a medium bowl, whisk together milk and egg. Place bread crumbs in a separate large bowl.
4. Dip onion rings into flour mixture to coat and set them aside. Pour milk mixture into the bowl of flour and stir to combine.
5. Dip onion rings into wet mixture and then press into bread crumbs to coat.
6. Place onion rings in the air fryer basket and spritz with cooking spray. Cook 12 minutes until the edges are crispy and golden. Serve warm.

PER SERVING

CALORIES: 250 | **FAT:** 3g | **PROTEIN:** 9g | **SODIUM:** 1,040mg | **FIBER:** 2g | **CARBOHYDRATES:** 46g | **SUGAR:** 5g

Ham and Cheese Sliders

No more long cooking times or having to tent your sliders with foil like with oven cooking. These sliders crisp up beautifully in just 10 minutes. The golden crust and gooey melted cheese make this a great appetizer for all ages.

Pantry Staples: none
Hands-On Time: 10 minutes
Cook Time: 10 minutes

Serves 3

- 6 Hawaiian sweet rolls
- 12 slices thinly sliced Black Forest ham
- 6 (1-ounce) slices sharp Cheddar cheese
- ¼ cup salted butter, melted
- 1½ teaspoons minced garlic

1. Preheat the air fryer to 350°F.
2. For each slider, slice horizontally through the center of a roll without fully separating the two halves. Place 2 slices ham and 2 slices cheese inside roll and close. Repeat with remaining rolls, ham, and cheese.
3. In a small bowl, mix butter and garlic and brush over all sides of rolls.
4. Place in the air fryer and cook 10 minutes until rolls are golden on top and cheese is melted. Serve warm.

PER SERVING (SERVING SIZE: 2 SLIDERS)

CALORIES: 860 | **FAT:** 42g | **PROTEIN:** 39g | **SODIUM:** 1,640mg | **FIBER:** 0g | **CARBOHYDRATES:** 82g | **SUGAR:** 16g

SPICY ITALIAN ALTERNATIVE

If ham and cheese aren't your thing, try using salami, pepperoni, and pepper jack cheese instead. Brush the tops of the rolls with Dijon or spicy mustard for an extra kick.

Bacon-Wrapped Jalapeño Poppers

This classic jalapeño poppers appetizer just got even more delicious. These poppers take on the flavor of smoky bacon, which also gives each popper a much-needed crunch. The inside is full of gooey cheese, which helps offset the spiciness of the pepper.

Pantry Staples: none
Hands-On Time: 10 minutes
Cook Time: 12 minutes

Serves 4

3 ounces full-fat cream cheese
½ cup shredded sharp Cheddar cheese
¼ teaspoon garlic powder
6 (4") jalapeño peppers, trimmed and halved lengthwise, seeded and membranes removed
12 slices bacon

1. Preheat the air fryer to 400°F.
2. In a large microwave-safe bowl, place cream cheese, Cheddar, and garlic powder. Microwave 20 seconds until softened and stir. Spoon cheese mixture into hollow jalapeño halves.
3. Wrap a bacon slice around each jalapeño half, completely covering pepper.
4. Place in the air fryer basket and cook 12 minutes, turning halfway through cooking time. Serve warm.

PER SERVING

CALORIES: 490 | **FAT:** 45g | **PROTEIN:** 16g | **SODIUM:** 710mg | **FIBER:** 1g | **CARBOHYDRATES:** 4g | **SUGAR:** 2g

Garlic–Cream Cheese Wontons

While many wontons have pork inside, this meat-free alternative might just be your new favorite. Whether you're enjoying these alone or with a meal, you'll be wishing you made a double batch.

Pantry Staples: none
Hands-On Time: 10 minutes
Cook Time: 8 minutes

Serves 4

6 ounces full-fat cream cheese, softened
1 teaspoon garlic powder
12 wonton wrappers
¼ cup water

1. Preheat the air fryer to 375°F.
2. In a medium bowl, mix cream cheese and garlic powder until smooth.
3. For each wonton, place 1 tablespoon cream cheese mixture in center of a wonton wrapper.
4. Brush edges of wonton with water to help it seal. Fold wonton to form a triangle. Spritz both sides with cooking spray. Repeat with remaining wontons and cream cheese mixture.
5. Place wontons in the air fryer basket. Cook 8 minutes, turning halfway through cooking time, until golden brown and crispy. Serve warm.

PER SERVING

CALORIES: 200 | **FAT:** 15g | **PROTEIN:** 5g | **SODIUM:** 250mg | **FIBER:** 0g | **CARBOHYDRATES:** 12g | **SUGAR:** 2g

Tortilla Chips

Whether you're dipping in guacamole, queso, or salsa, this recipe gives you the easiest way to make delicious Tortilla Chips at home. These can even be reheated by cooking 3 minutes in the air fryer at 120°F to make like fresh again.

Pantry Staples: salt
Hands-On Time: 5 minutes
Cook Time: 5 minutes per batch

Serves 4

8 (6") white corn tortillas
¼ cup olive oil
2 tablespoons lime juice
½ teaspoon salt

1. Preheat the air fryer to 350°F.
2. Cut each tortilla into fourths and brush lightly with oil.
3. Place chips in a single layer in the air fryer basket, working in batches as necessary. Cook 5 minutes, shaking the basket halfway through cooking time.
4. Sprinkle with lime juice and salt. Serve warm.

PER SERVING

CALORIES: 230 | **FAT:** 15g | **PROTEIN:** 2g | **SODIUM:** 300mg | **FIBER:** 0g | **CARBOHYDRATES:** 24g | **SUGAR:** 2g

Spinach Dip

Whether you like to dip pretzels or pita, this deliciously creamy dip is for you. This classic has all the cheesy flavor you'll love. If you like your dip to have a little heat, try adding a teaspoon of crushed red pepper flakes before cooking.

Pantry Staples: none
Hands-On Time: 10 minutes
Cook Time: 15 minutes

Yield 2 cups

8 ounces full-fat cream cheese, softened
½ cup mayonnaise
2 teaspoons minced garlic
1 cup grated Parmesan cheese
1 (10-ounce) package frozen chopped spinach, thawed and drained

1. Preheat the air fryer to 320°F.
2. In a large bowl, mix cream cheese, mayonnaise, garlic, and Parmesan.
3. Fold in spinach. Scrape mixture into a 6" round baking dish and place in the air fryer basket.
4. Cook 15 minutes until mixture is bubbling and top begins to turn brown. Serve warm.

PER SERVING (SERVING SIZE: ¼ CUP)

CALORIES: 250 | **FAT:** 23g | **PROTEIN:** 6g | **SODIUM:** 390mg | **FIBER:** 1g | **CARBOHYDRATES:** 4g | **SUGAR:** 1g

Corn Dog Bites

There's no need to buy frozen corn dog bites when you can easily make them at home now without dealing with hot oil. The air fryer gives the bites a beautiful dark golden crust just like your favorite frozen brand. These bites are crispy on the outside and juicy on the inside with just a subtle hint of sweetness that will keep you coming back for more.

Pantry Staples: all-purpose flour, granulated sugar, baking powder
Hands-On Time: 30 minutes
Cook Time: 10 minutes per batch

Serves 6

- ½ cup cornmeal
- ¾ cup all-purpose flour
- ½ cup whole milk
- 1 large egg
- 2 tablespoons granulated sugar
- 2 teaspoons baking powder
- 6 beef hot dogs

1. Cut parchment paper to fit the air fryer basket.
2. In a large bowl, mix cornmeal, flour, milk, egg, sugar, and baking powder. Let mixture sit 5 minutes to thicken.
3. Cut each hot dog into four equal pieces.
4. Using a skewer or fork, dip hot dog pieces into cornmeal mixture. Place carefully on a plate.
5. Preheat the air fryer to 375°F.
6. Chill corn dog bites in freezer 10 minutes. Place on parchment in the air fryer basket, working in batches as necessary, and cook 10 minutes, turning halfway through cooking time, until golden brown. Serve warm.

PER SERVING (SERVING SIZE: 4 BITES)

CALORIES: 290 | **FAT:** 16g | **PROTEIN:** 10g | **SODIUM:** 440mg | **FIBER:** 1g | **CARBOHYDRATES:** 26g | **SUGAR:** 6g

Cheese Crackers

These homemade Cheese Crackers are packed with flavor and use much simpler ingredients than the ones you'll find in the store. The crackers puff up and deliver a light and airy Cheddar crunch in every bite. Make a batch ahead of time for an easy after-school snack.

Pantry Staples: all-purpose flour, salt
Hands-On Time: 20 minutes
Cook Time: 10 minutes per batch

Serves 4

4 ounces sharp Cheddar cheese, shredded
½ cup all-purpose flour
2 tablespoons salted butter, cubed
½ teaspoon salt
2 tablespoons cold water

1. In a large bowl, using an electric hand mixer, mix all ingredients until dough forms. Pack dough together into a ball and wrap tightly in plastic wrap. Chill in the freezer 15 minutes.
2. Preheat the air fryer to 375°F. Cut parchment paper to fit the air fryer basket.
3. Spread a separate large sheet of parchment paper on a work surface. Remove dough from the freezer and roll out ¼" thick on parchment paper. Use a pizza cutter to cut dough into 1" squares.
4. Place crackers on precut parchment in the air fryer basket and cook 10 minutes, working in batches as necessary.
5. Allow crackers to cool at least 10 minutes before serving.

PER SERVING

CALORIES: 220 | **FAT:** 15g | **PROTEIN:** 9g | **SODIUM:** 520mg | **FIBER:** 1g | **CARBOHYDRATES:** 13g | **SUGAR:** 0g

MAKE IT YOUR OWN

Adding your favorite herbs and spices is a great way to add flavor. Try adding ½ teaspoon chili powder and ¼ teaspoon garlic powder for a little spice or even ½ teaspoon dried rosemary. You can also add a sprinkle of your favorite premade spice mixes.

Roasted Red Salsa

Homemade salsa is easy to make and customize to your favorite flavors. The most important thing is finding deep red, ripe, juicy tomatoes for the base because they will set the flavor for the whole dish. Roasting the vegetables allows them to caramelize and adds a whole new flavor to your salsa.

Pantry Staples: salt
Hands-On Time: 5 minutes
Cook Time: 10 minutes

Yields 1 cup

10 medium Roma tomatoes, quartered
1 medium white onion, peeled and sliced
2 medium cloves garlic, peeled
2 tablespoons olive oil
¼ cup chopped fresh cilantro
½ teaspoon salt

1. Preheat the air fryer to 340°F.
2. Place tomatoes, onion, and garlic into a 6" round baking dish. Drizzle with oil and toss to coat.
3. Place in the air fryer basket and cook 10 minutes, stirring twice during cooking, until vegetables start to turn dark brown and caramelize.
4. In a food processor, add roasted vegetables, cilantro, and salt. Pulse five times until vegetables are mostly broken down. Serve immediately.

PER SERVING (SERVING SIZE: ¼ CUP)

CALORIES: 100 | **FAT:** 7g | **PROTEIN:** 2g | **SODIUM:** 300mg | **FIBER:** 2g | **CARBOHYDRATES:** 9g | **SUGAR:** 5g

MAKE IT YOUR OWN

Try roasting a fresh jalapeño pepper with the vegetables for a spicier salsa. For a milder taste you can use chopped green chilies. You can also add a splash of lime juice to add brightness to this dish.

Buffalo Chicken Dip

This tangy dip takes only 10 minutes in the air fryer, making it easier than ever to make. It's perfect for enjoying with chips and even goes great with chopped vegetables like carrots and celery. This recipe calls for precooked chicken, which makes it a perfect use for leftovers. You can also use canned chicken or a rotisserie chicken to save time.

Pantry Staples: none
Hands-On Time: 10 minutes
Cook Time: 10 minutes

Yield 2 cups

- **4 ounces full-fat cream cheese, softened**
- **½ teaspoon garlic powder**
- **½ cup buffalo sauce**
- **1 cup shredded Cheddar cheese, divided**
- **2 cups cooked and shredded chicken breast**

1. Preheat the air fryer to 350°F.
2. In a large bowl, mix cream cheese, garlic powder, buffalo sauce, and ½ cup Cheddar until well combined. Fold in chicken until well coated.
3. Scrape mixture into a 6" round baking dish and top with remaining ½ cup Cheddar.
4. Place dish in the air fryer basket and cook 10 minutes until top is brown and edges are bubbling. Serve warm.

PER SERVING (SERVING SIZE: ¼ CUP)

CALORIES: 140 | **FAT:** 10g | **PROTEIN:** 12g | **SODIUM:** 190mg | **FIBER:** 0g | **CARBOHYDRATES:** 1g | **SUGAR:** 1g

Greek Turkey Meatballs

This juicy, delicious dish is the perfect way to change up your usual meatballs. Turkey can be a great alternative to red meat. This recipe is packed with fresh ingredients that will elevate your ground turkey and make it a meal everyone will love. Try dipping these meatballs into tzatziki sauce or enjoying them alongside pita bread for a complete meal.

Pantry Staples: salt, ground black pepper
Hands-On Time: 15 minutes
Cook Time: 15 minutes per batch

Serves 5

- **1 pound 85/15 ground turkey**
- **1 cup chopped fresh spinach**
- **½ cup diced red onion**
- **½ cup crumbled feta cheese**
- **½ cup bread crumbs**
- **½ teaspoon salt**
- **¼ teaspoon ground black pepper**

1. Preheat the air fryer to 350°F.
2. In a large bowl, mix all ingredients until well combined.
3. Roll mixture into balls, about 1 heaping tablespoon for each, to make twenty meatballs.
4. Spritz with cooking spray and place in the air fryer basket, working in batches as necessary. Cook 15 minutes, shaking the basket three times during cooking time, until golden brown and internal temperature reaches at least 165°F. Serve warm.

PER SERVING (SERVING SIZE: 4 MEATBALLS)

CALORIES: 280 | **FAT:** 17g | **PROTEIN:** 19g | **SODIUM:** 520mg | **FIBER:** 0g | **CARBOHYDRATES:** 10g | **SUGAR:** 2g

APPETIZER BITES

These flavorful meatballs make great mini bites for a party. Use a cocktail toothpick to place a cherry tomato and a ¼" slice of cucumber on each to make small skewers. Arrange on a platter and place a bowl of tzatziki sauce in the center for dipping.

Mozzarella Sticks

This classic appetizer is now even easier in the air fryer. You'll need to plan ahead to allow for freezing time, but they're definitely worth the wait. This recipe uses panko bread crumbs, which give the sticks the ultimate crunch and flavor. Serve with warm marinara sauce topped with Parmesan cheese for a restaurant-worthy appetizer.

Pantry Staples: all-purpose flour, salt
Hands-On Time: 10 minutes
Cook Time: 2 hours 5 minutes

Serves 4

12 (1-ounce) sticks mozzarella string cheese
1 cup all-purpose flour
4 large eggs, beaten
2½ cups panko bread crumbs
2½ teaspoons Italian seasoning
½ teaspoon salt

1. Cut mozzarella sticks in half crosswise. Place in an airtight freezer-safe bag and freeze at least 1 hour.
2. In three separate bowls, place flour, eggs, and bread crumbs. Add Italian seasoning and salt to the bowl with bread crumbs and stir to combine.
3. Remove mozzarella sticks from freezer. Dip each stick in flour and shake off the excess. Then, dip in eggs, letting excess drip off, and finally, dip in bread crumbs to coat. Dip again in eggs, dripping off excess, and again in bread crumbs, so that mozzarella stick is double coated. Repeat with remaining mozzarella sticks.
4. Place coated cheese sticks on a plate and return them to the freezer at least 1 hour.
5. Preheat the air fryer to 400°F.
6. Spray each cheese stick with cooking spray. Place in the air fryer basket in a single layer, working in batches as necessary, and cook 5 minutes. Let cool 5 minutes before serving.

PER SERVING

CALORIES: 600 | **FAT:** 23g | **PROTEIN:** 36g | **SODIUM:** 1,080mg | **FIBER:** 1g | **CARBOHYDRATES:** 62g | **SUGAR:** 1g

Pork Egg Rolls

Whether you're enjoying this dish as an entrée or appetizer, it's always a crowd favorite. The air fryer allows you to skip the hot oil and still get golden, crispy egg rolls. Broccoli slaw is mild tasting and crunchier than the traditional cabbage filling. It adds extra crunch that takes these egg rolls to a whole new level.

Pantry Staples: salt
Hands-On Time: 10 minutes
Cook Time: 17 minutes

Serves 4

- **½ pound 84% lean ground pork**
- **3 tablespoons low-sodium soy sauce, divided**
- **½ teaspoon salt**
- **2 cups broccoli slaw**
- **½ teaspoon ground ginger**
- **8 egg roll wrappers**

1. In a medium skillet over medium heat, crumble ground pork and cook about 10 minutes until fully cooked and no pink remains. Drain fat and return meat to skillet.
2. Pour 2 tablespoons soy sauce over pork, then sprinkle with salt and stir. Reduce heat to low and cook 2 minutes.
3. Add broccoli slaw. Pour remaining soy sauce over broccoli slaw and sprinkle with ginger. Stir and continue cooking 5 minutes until slaw is tender.
4. Preheat the air fryer to 350°F.
5. For each egg roll, position a wrapper so that one corner is pointed toward you. Spoon 3 tablespoons pork mixture across the wrapper near the corner closest to you.
6. Roll the point closest to you over the filling. Fold the left and right corners toward the center, then roll the wrapper closed toward the far corner. Repeat with remaining wrappers and filling.
7. Place in the air fryer basket seam side down and cook 10 minutes, turning halfway through cooking time. Serve warm.

PER SERVING (SERVING SIZE: 2 ROLLS)

CALORIES: 260 | **FAT:** 9g | **PROTEIN:** 17g | **SODIUM:** 1,050mg | **FIBER:** 0g | **CARBOHYDRATES:** 27g | **SUGAR:** 2g

Beef Taco–Stuffed Meatballs

Instead of traditional tacos, try this flavor-packed recipe that's perfect for meal prep. These meatballs are loaded with taco flavor. The gooey cheese center will take this recipe to the next level, helping it become a family favorite.

Pantry Staples: none
Hands-On Time: 25 minutes
Cook Time: 15 minutes

Serves 6

4 ounces Colby jack cheese cut into ½" cubes
1 pound 80/20 ground beef
1 (1-ounce) packet taco seasoning
½ cup bread crumbs

1. Preheat the air fryer to 350°F. Chill cheese in the freezer 15 minutes.
2. In a large bowl, mix beef, taco seasoning, and bread crumbs. Roll mixture into balls, about 2" each, to make eighteen meatballs.
3. Remove cheese from freezer. Place one cube into each meatball by pressing gently into the center and shaping meat around cheese. Roll into a ball.
4. Spritz meatballs with cooking spray and place in the air fryer basket. Cook 15 minutes, shaking the basket three times during cooking, until meatballs are brown and internal temperature has reached at least 165°F. Serve warm.

PER SERVING (SERVING SIZE: 3 MEATBALLS)

CALORIES: 310 | **FAT:** 21g | **PROTEIN:** 18g | **SODIUM:** 620mg | **FIBER:** 0g | **CARBOHYDRATES:** 10g | **SUGAR:** 1g

SERVING IDEA

Make these meatballs a fun dinner by setting them out with a variety of sauces. Place toothpicks in the meatballs and place bowls of sour cream, salsa, warm queso, and guacamole around the platter so everyone can enjoy their favorite sauce.

Croutons

There's no need to waste your extra bread—simply turn it into a golden bite that's perfect for any salad. These crispy Croutons cook up in just a few minutes.

Pantry Staples: none
Hands-On Time: 5 minutes
Cook Time: 5 minutes

Serves 4

4 slices sourdough bread, diced into small cubes
2 tablespoons salted butter, melted
1 teaspoon chopped fresh parsley
2 tablespoons grated Parmesan cheese

1 Preheat the air fryer to 400°F.
2 Place bread cubes in a large bowl.
3 Pour butter over bread cubes. Add parsley and Parmesan. Toss bread cubes until evenly coated.
4 Place bread cubes in the air fryer basket in a single layer. Cook 5 minutes until well toasted. Serve cooled for maximum crunch.

PER SERVING

CALORIES: 440 | **FAT:** 10g | **PROTEIN:** 16g | **SODIUM:** 930mg | **FIBER:** 0g | **CARBOHYDRATES:** 72g | **SUGAR:** 6g

Pigs in a Blanket

This childhood classic is an air fryer must. It's perfect for those days when you need a quick meal without much prep.

Pantry Staples: none
Hands-On Time: 5 minutes
Cook Time: 10 minutes

Serves 8

1 (8-ounce) can crescent rolls
8 jumbo beef hot dogs
1 large egg, whisked
1 tablespoon sesame seeds

1 Preheat the air fryer to 350°F.
2 Separate crescent rolls into eight triangles and place a hot dog on top of each.
3 Roll hot dog into crescent roll, beginning at the widest end and rolling toward the smallest.
4 Brush each roll with egg and sprinkle with sesame seeds, pressing them gently into place.
5 Place in the air fryer basket and cook 10 minutes, turning halfway through cooking time. Crescent rolls will be golden brown and hot dogs brown when done. Serve warm.

PER SERVING

CALORIES: 380 | **FAT:** 31g | **PROTEIN:** 12g | **SODIUM:** 1,040mg | **FIBER:** 0g | **CARBOHYDRATES:** 14g | **SUGAR:** 3g

Potato Skins

This crispy and cheesy appetizer is always a crowd pleaser. The best thing about this recipe is that you can top it any way you like. Feel free to add bacon, extra cheese, or even a dash of hot sauce. You won't need the scooped-out potato flesh for this recipe, so you can use it for the Fried Mashed Potato Balls in Chapter 4.

Pantry Staples: salt, ground black pepper
Hands-On Time: 15 minutes
Cook Time: 35 minutes per batch

Serves 4

4 large russet potatoes
½ cup shredded sharp Cheddar cheese
1 teaspoon salt
½ teaspoon ground black pepper
½ cup sour cream
1 medium green onion, sliced

1. Preheat the air fryer to 400°F.
2. Using a fork, poke several holes in potatoes. Place potatoes in the air fryer basket and cook 30 minutes until fork tender.
3. Once potatoes are cool enough to handle, slice them in half lengthwise and scoop out the insides, being careful to maintain the structural integrity of the potato skins. Reserve potato flesh for another use.
4. Sprinkle insides of potato skins with Cheddar, salt, and pepper. Working in batches if needed, place back in the air fryer basket and cook 5 minutes until cheese is melted and bubbling.
5. Let cool 5 minutes, then top with sour cream and green onion. Serve.

PER SERVING

CALORIES: 270 | **FAT:** 10g | **PROTEIN:** 9g | **SODIUM:** 710mg | **FIBER:** 3g | **CARBOHYDRATES:** 41g | **SUGAR:** 2g

Buffalo Chicken Wings

These crispy, spicy, mouthwatering wings are an absolute must for any game day gathering. Pair them with blue cheese dressing or ranch to help cool down the spice and keep the party going.

Pantry Staples: salt, ground black pepper
Hands-On Time: 5 minutes
Cook Time: 20 minutes per batch

Serves 4

2 pounds chicken wings, flats and drums separated
1 teaspoon salt
½ teaspoon ground black pepper
¼ cup salted butter, melted
¼ cup hot sauce

1. Preheat the air fryer to 375°F.
2. Sprinkle wings with salt and pepper. Place wings in a single layer in the air fryer basket, working in batches as necessary.
3. Cook 20 minutes, turning halfway through cooking time, until wings are golden and crispy and internal temperature reaches at least 165°F.
4. While wings are cooking, in a medium bowl, combine butter and hot sauce. Toss cooked wings in sauce until well coated. Serve.

PER SERVING

CALORIES: 340 | **FAT:** 27g | **PROTEIN:** 22g | **SODIUM:** 1,150mg | **FIBER:** 0g | **CARBOHYDRATES:** 0g | **SUGAR:** 0g

Korean-Style Wings

These deep brown red wings are packed with spices, savory elements, and a great crunch. This sauce is made with gochujang, which is a Korean chili sauce. It has a sweet heat and lots of flavor. You can find this in the international foods section at the grocery store. If you'd like, garnish these with a sprinkle of parsley for a fancy presentation.

Pantry Staples: salt, ground black pepper
Hands-On Time: 5 minutes
Cook Time: 20 minutes

Serves 4

1 pound chicken wings, drums and flats separated
½ teaspoon salt
¼ teaspoon ground black pepper
¼ cup gochujang sauce
2 tablespoons soy sauce
1 teaspoon ground ginger
¼ cup mayonnaise

1. Preheat the air fryer to 350°F.
2. Sprinkle wings with salt and pepper. Place wings in the air fryer basket and cook 15 minutes, turning halfway through cooking time.
3. In a medium bowl, mix gochujang sauce, soy sauce, ginger, and mayonnaise.
4. Toss wings in sauce mixture and adjust the air fryer temperature to 400°F.
5. Place wings back in the air fryer basket and cook an additional 5 minutes until the internal temperature reaches at least 165°F. Serve warm.

PER SERVING

CALORIES: 260 | **FAT:** 19g | **PROTEIN:** 12g | **SODIUM:** 1,360mg | **FIBER:** 0g | **CARBOHYDRATES:** 11g | **SUGAR:** 6g

Fried Pickles

This tangy appetizer is delicious and easy to make. It has both a big crunch and lots of flavor. Try dipping the pickles in ranch or even enjoying on top of a burger for a fun twist.

Pantry Staples: all-purpose flour
Hands-On Time: 5 minutes
Cook Time: 10 minutes

Serves 4

20 dill pickle slices
1 cup plain bread crumbs
2 teaspoons seasoned salt
½ cup all-purpose flour
2 large eggs, whisked

1. Preheat the air fryer to 350°F. Set pickles on a paper towel to absorb excess moisture.
2. In a medium bowl, combine bread crumbs and seasoned salt. In a separate medium bowl, place flour. In a third medium bowl, place eggs.
3. Dredge a pickle slice in flour. Shake off excess and dip in eggs. Shake off excess and dip in bread crumbs. Repeat with remaining pickle slices. Place in a single layer in the air fryer basket.
4. Spritz with cooking spray and cook 10 minutes until golden brown and crispy. Serve.

PER SERVING (SERVING SIZE: 5 PICKLES)

CALORIES: 200 | **FAT:** 4g | **PROTEIN:** 9g | **SODIUM:** 1,090mg | **FIBER:** 1g | **CARBOHYDRATES:** 32g | **SUGAR:** 1g

Apple Chips

These Apple Chips are the perfect healthy snack, flavored lightly with cinnamon and no added sugar.

Pantry Staples: none
Hands-On Time: 5 minutes
Cook Time: 15 minutes per batch

Serves 4

2 large Granny Smith apples, cored and sliced ⅛" thick
¼ teaspoon ground cinnamon

1. Preheat the air fryer to 300°F. Spray apple slices with cooking spray and place them in a single layer in the air fryer basket, working in batches as necessary.
2. Lightly sprinkle with cinnamon and cook 15 minutes.
3. Let apple chips cool and continue to crisp up for 5 minutes before serving.

PER SERVING

CALORIES: 60 | **FAT:** 0g | **PROTEIN:** 0g | **SODIUM:** 0mg | **FIBER:** 3g | **CARBOHYDRATES:** 14g | **SUGAR:** 10g

4

Side Dishes

Sides are important to creating a satisfying, well-rounded meal. And sometimes sides can steal the show. What's a Thanksgiving turkey without the mashed potatoes? Can you really fully enjoy a cheeseburger without fries on the side? But sides can also be a daunting kitchen task, especially with all the effort that goes into crafting the perfect entrée. The good news is your air fryer is ready to rise to the occasion. From Macaroni and Cheese to Sweet Potato Fries, this chapter is full of easy ideas to round out your meal in a delicious and complete way.

Flaky Biscuits

There's nothing quite like biting into a warm, flaky biscuit. That's why they're such a popular side at so many fast-food restaurants. Now you can recreate the popular taste in a way that's much better than the refrigerated dough. Drizzle some honey on top to make them extra special!

Pantry Staples: salt
Hands-On Time: 10 minutes
Cook Time: 15 minutes per batch

Serves 8

¼ cup salted butter
2 cups self-rising flour
¼ teaspoon salt
⅔ cup whole milk

COLD BUTTER

The flakiest biscuits are made with cold, almost frozen, butter. This makes for little pockets of air that give the biscuit rise. If you use warm or melted butter, you're more likely to end up with dense, chewy biscuits.

1. Preheat the air fryer to 320°F. Cut parchment paper to fit the air fryer basket.
2. Place butter in the freezer 10 minutes. In a large bowl, mix flour and salt.
3. Grate butter into bowl and use a wooden spoon to evenly distribute. Add milk and stir until a soft dough forms.
4. Turn dough onto a lightly floured surface. Gently press and flatten dough until mostly smooth and uniform. Gently roll into an 8" × 10" rectangle. Use a sharp knife dusted in flour to cut dough into eight squares.
5. Place biscuits on parchment paper in the air fryer basket, working in batches as necessary, and cook 15 minutes until golden brown on the top and edges and feel firm to the touch. Let cool 5 minutes before serving.

PER SERVING

CALORIES: 170 | **FAT:** 6g | **PROTEIN:** 4g | **SODIUM:** 520mg | **FIBER:** 1g | **CARBOHYDRATES:** 24g | **SUGAR:** 1g

Sweet Potato Fries

Sweet potatoes are a great way to switch up your fry routine. They have more natural sugars than white potatoes, which allows the edges to get crispy and caramelized. If you love sweet and savory, you'll love this recipe.

Pantry Staples: salt
Hands-On Time: 5 minutes
Cook Time: 40 minutes

Serves 4

- **2 large sweet potatoes, trimmed and sliced into ¼" × 4" sticks**
- **1 tablespoon olive oil**
- **½ teaspoon salt**

1. Place sweet potato sticks in a large bowl of cold water and let soak 30 minutes.
2. Preheat the air fryer to 380°F.
3. Drain potatoes and gently pat dry. Place in a large, dry bowl. Drizzle with oil and sprinkle with salt, then toss to fully coat.
4. Place fries in the air fryer basket and cook 10 minutes, shaking the basket three times during cooking, until fries are tender and golden brown.
5. Serve warm.

PER SERVING

CALORIES: 120 | **FAT:** 7g | **PROTEIN:** 1g | **SODIUM:** 330mg | **FIBER:** 2g | **CARBOHYDRATES:** 13g | **SUGAR:** 3g

ADD SOME KICK

To add some extra flavor, try mixing ½ cup ketchup with 1 tablespoon sriracha for a smoky and spicy dipping sauce.

Garlic-Parmesan French Fries

French fries are classic, but there's never any harm in bringing them to the next level with new, mouthwatering seasonings. These golden, crispy fries are coated in fragrant garlic and finished with fresh cheese to give this side a restaurant-style quality that everyone will love.

Pantry Staples: salt, ground black pepper
Hands-On Time: 5 minutes
Cook Time: 45 minutes

Serves 4

3 large russet potatoes, peeled, trimmed, and sliced into ½" × 4" sticks
2½ tablespoons olive oil, divided
2 teaspoons minced garlic
½ teaspoon salt
¼ teaspoon ground black pepper
1 teaspoon dried parsley
¼ cup grated Parmesan cheese

1. Place potato sticks in a large bowl of cold water and let soak 30 minutes.
2. Preheat the air fryer to 350°F.
3. Drain potatoes and gently pat dry. Place in a large, dry bowl.
4. Pour 2 tablespoons oil over potatoes. Add garlic, salt, and pepper, then toss to fully coat.
5. Place fries in the air fryer basket and cook 15 minutes, shaking the basket twice during cooking, until fries are golden and crispy on the edges.
6. Place fries into a clean medium bowl and drizzle with remaining ½ tablespoon oil. Sprinkle parsley and Parmesan over fries and toss to coat. Serve warm.

PER SERVING

CALORIES: 230 | **FAT:** 10g | **PROTEIN:** 5g | **SODIUM:** 380mg | **FIBER:** 2g | **CARBOHYDRATES:** 30g | **SUGAR:** 1g

Potato Wedges

This classic side cooks even faster than usual in the air fryer. Its golden and crispy exterior is the perfect companion to any steak or burger meal. The dredging gives them extra crunch, making them perfect for scooping up sauces like creamy honey mustard.

Pantry Staples: all-purpose flour
Hands-On Time: 10 minutes
Cook Time: 20 minutes

Serves 4

6 cups water
4 large russet potatoes, sliced into wedges
2 teaspoons seasoned salt
½ cup whole milk
½ cup all-purpose flour

SHORT ON TIME?

If you don't have time to boil the potatoes, leave them whole and prick them with a fork all over, then microwave on high 4 minutes. This will soften them enough to cut and cook up quickly in the air fryer.

1. In a large saucepan over medium-high heat, bring water to a boil.
2. Carefully place potato wedges into boiling water and cook 5 minutes.
3. Preheat the air fryer to 400°F.
4. Drain potatoes into a colander, then rinse under cold running water 1 minute until they feel cool to the touch.
5. Place potatoes in a large bowl and sprinkle with seasoned salt. Pour milk into bowl, then toss wedges to coat.
6. Place flour on a large plate. Gently dredge each potato wedge in flour on both sides to lightly coat.
7. Place wedges in the air fryer basket and spritz both sides with cooking spray. Cook 15 minutes, turning after 10 minutes, until wedges are golden brown. Serve warm.

PER SERVING

CALORIES: 240 | **FAT:** 1g | **PROTEIN:** 9g | **SODIUM:** 670mg | **FIBER:** 4g | **CARBOHYDRATES:** 53g | **SUGAR:** 3g

Garlic Knots

These knots will be a hit with kids and adults alike. There's no waiting for dough to rise since this version doesn't utilize yeast. This recipe creates a bready, soft, and golden appetizer perfect for any night of the week in about 20 minutes. Feel free to add a sprinkle of Italian seasoning for even more flavor.

Pantry Staples: none
Hands-On Time: 10 minutes
Cook Time: 15 minutes

Serves 5

1 cup self-rising flour
1 cup plain full-fat Greek yogurt
⅓ cup salted butter, melted
1 teaspoon garlic powder
¼ cup grated Parmesan cheese

1. Preheat the air fryer to 320°F.
2. In a large bowl, mix flour and yogurt and let sit 5 minutes.
3. Turn dough onto a lightly floured surface and gently knead about 3 minutes until it's no longer sticky.
4. Form dough into a rectangle and roll out until it measures 10" × 6". Cut dough into ten 1"× 6" strips.
5. Tie each dough strip into a knot. Brush each knot with butter and sprinkle with garlic powder.
6. Place in the air fryer basket and cook 8 minutes, turning after 6 minutes. Let cool 2 min utes, sprinkle with Parmesan, and serve.

PER SERVING (SERVING SIZE: 2 KNOTS)

CALORIES: 270 | **FAT:** 16g | **PROTEIN:** 9g | **SODIUM:** 500mg | **FIBER:** 1g | **CARBOHYDRATES:** 22g | **SUGAR:** 2g

Corn Muffins

The best corn muffins have golden, crispy edges and a hint of sweetness. The air fryer gives these the perfect crust on top. Pair these with a pat of butter or drizzle of honey.

Pantry Staples: all-purpose flour, granulated sugar, baking powder
Hands-On Time: 5 minutes
Cook Time: 10 minutes

Serves 12

½ cup all-purpose flour
½ cup cornmeal
¼ cup granulated sugar
½ teaspoon baking powder
¼ cup salted butter, melted
½ cup buttermilk
1 large egg

1. Preheat the air fryer to 350°F.
2. In a large bowl, whisk together flour, cornmeal, sugar, and baking powder.
3. Add butter, buttermilk, and egg to dry mixture. Stir until well combined.
4. Divide batter evenly among twelve silicone or aluminum muffin cups, filling cups about halfway. Working in batches as needed, place in the air fryer and cook 10 minutes until golden brown. Let cool 5 minutes before serving.

PER SERVING (SERVING SIZE: 1 MUFFIN)

CALORIES: 100 | **FAT:** 5g | **PROTEIN:** 2g | **SODIUM:** 45mg | **FIBER:** 1g | **CARBOHYDRATES:** 12g | **SUGAR:** 5g

Macaroni and Cheese

Yes, you can prepare macaroni and cheese from scratch completely in your air fryer. The result is just like your favorite cheesy, gooey stovetop mac and cheese, and it requires just a few stirs to ensure even cooking. Try adding an extra ½ cup of your favorite shredded cheese, such as Gouda or Colby. Feel free to top with bread crumbs or bacon for serving.

Pantry Staples: ground black pepper
Hands-On Time: 5 minutes
Cook Time: 25 minutes

Serves 4

1½ cups dry elbow macaroni
1 cup chicken broth
½ cup whole milk
2 tablespoons salted butter, melted
8 ounces sharp Cheddar cheese, shredded, divided
½ teaspoon ground black pepper

1. Preheat the air fryer to 350°F.
2. In a 6" baking dish, combine macaroni, broth, milk, butter, half the Cheddar, and pepper. Stir to combine.
3. Place in the air fryer basket and cook 12 minutes.
4. Stir in remaining Cheddar, then return the basket to the air fryer and cook 13 additional minutes.
5. Stir macaroni and cheese until creamy. Let cool 10 minutes before serving.

PER SERVING

CALORIES: 500 | **FAT:** 26g | **PROTEIN:** 22g | **SODIUM:** 660mg | **FIBER:** 0g | **CARBOHYDRATES:** 46g | **SUGAR:** 4g

Roasted Broccoli

Roasting vegetables allows their natural sweetness to really shine. This simple dish is perfect for last-minute meal additions. The edges of the broccoli get crispy and golden with a hint of sweetness while the rest remains fork-tender.

Pantry Staples: salt, ground black pepper
Hands-On Time: 5 minutes
Cook Time: 8 minutes

Serves 4

12 ounces broccoli florets
2 tablespoons olive oil
½ teaspoon salt
¼ teaspoon ground black pepper

1. Preheat the air fryer to 360°F.
2. In a medium bowl, place broccoli and drizzle with oil. Sprinkle with salt and pepper.
3. Place in the air fryer basket and cook 8 minutes, shaking the basket twice during cooking, until the edges are brown and the center is tender. Serve warm.

PER SERVING

CALORIES: 80 | **FAT:** 7g | **PROTEIN:** 3g | **SODIUM:** 310mg | **FIBER:** 2g | **CARBOHYDRATES:** 4g | **SUGAR:** 1g

Sweet Butternut Squash

This side dish is perfect for squash lovers. Caramelized edges and a little added sugar accentuate the natural sweetness of the squash. This delicious dish is easy to make and adds some variety to any meal.

Pantry Staples: salt
Hands-On Time: 10 minutes
Cook Time: 15 minutes

Serves 8

1 medium butternut squash, peeled and cubed (about 2½ cups)
2 tablespoons salted butter, melted
½ teaspoon salt
1½ tablespoons brown sugar
½ teaspoon ground cinnamon

1. Preheat the air fryer to 400°F.
2. In a large bowl, place squash and add butter. Toss to coat. Sprinkle salt, brown sugar, and cinnamon over squash and toss to fully coat.
3. Place squash in the air fryer basket and cook 15 minutes, shaking the basket three times during cooking, until the edges are golden and the center is fork-tender. Serve warm.

PER SERVING

CALORIES: 60 | **FAT:** 3g | **PROTEIN:** 0g | **SODIUM:** 170mg | **FIBER:** 1g | **CARBOHYDRATES:** 8g | **SUGAR:** 4g

Savory Roasted Carrots

Side dishes don't have to take a lot of extra time. Premade seasoning powders offer a lot of flavor and convenience. If you love tender, buttery carrots, you'll definitely find yourself adding this delicious and easy dish to your weekly menu.

Pantry Staples: none
Hands-On Time: 5 minutes
Cook Time: 12 minutes

Serves 4

- **1 pound baby carrots**
- **2 tablespoons dry ranch seasoning**
- **3 tablespoons salted butter, melted**

1. Preheat the air fryer to 360°F.
2. Place carrots into a 6" round baking dish. Sprinkle carrots with ranch seasoning and drizzle with butter. Gently toss to coat.
3. Place in the air fryer basket and cook 12 minutes, stirring twice during cooking, until carrots are tender. Serve warm.

PER SERVING

CALORIES: 120 | **FAT:** 9g | **PROTEIN:** 1g | **SODIUM:** 190mg | **FIBER:** 3g | **CARBOHYDRATES:** 11g | **SUGAR:** 7g

Sweet Roasted Carrots

Sweet caramelized carrots are a great addition to savory meals. Carrots are naturally sweet, so the added sugar simply brightens them up and gives them a dark brown coating that makes each bite extra flavorful.

Pantry Staples: salt, ground black pepper
Hands-On Time: 5 minutes
Cook Time: 12 minutes

Serves 4

- **1 pound baby carrots**
- **¼ cup brown sugar**
- **2 tablespoons salted butter, melted**
- **¼ teaspoon garlic powder**
- **½ teaspoon salt**
- **¼ teaspoon ground black pepper**

1. Preheat the air fryer to 360°F.
2. Place carrots into a 6" round baking dish.
3. In a small bowl, mix brown sugar, butter, and garlic powder. Pour mixture over carrots and carefully stir to coat. Sprinkle with salt and pepper.
4. Place in the air fryer basket and cook 12 minutes, stirring three times during cooking, until carrots are tender. Serve warm.

PER SERVING

CALORIES: 150 | **FAT:** 6g | **PROTEIN:** 1g | **SODIUM:** 420mg | **FIBER:** 3g | **CARBOHYDRATES:** 23g | **SUGAR:** 19g

Brussels Sprouts

If you've never liked Brussels sprouts, roasting them might just change your mind. They're naturally sweet and flavorful, becoming crispy on the edges and buttery tender in the center. Roasting gives them a different flavor than boiling offers, and with how easy this tasty dish is, you might find yourself wishing you'd tried them sooner.

Pantry Staples: salt, ground black pepper
Hands-On Time: 5 minutes
Cook Time: 15 minutes

Serves 4

- 1 pound Brussels sprouts, trimmed and halved
- 2 tablespoons olive oil
- ½ teaspoon salt
- ¼ teaspoon ground black pepper

1. Preheat the air fryer to 350°F.
2. In a large bowl, place Brussels sprouts and drizzle with oil. Sprinkle with salt and pepper. Place in the air fryer basket and cook 15 minutes, shaking the basket three times during cooking. Serve warm.

PER SERVING

CALORIES: 110 | **FAT:** 7g | **PROTEIN:** 4g | **SODIUM:** 320mg | **FIBER:** 4g | **CARBOHYDRATES:** 10g | **SUGAR:** 2g

Fried Mashed Potato Balls

This recipe is great to make from scratch, but it's also an excellent way to repurpose your leftover mashed potatoes. These are golden and crispy on the outside and filled with delicious melted cheese on the inside.

Pantry Staples: salt, ground black pepper
Hands-On Time: 15 minutes
Cook Time: 10 minutes

Serves 4

- 2 cups mashed potatoes (about 4 medium russet potatoes)
- ¾ cup sour cream, divided
- 1 teaspoon salt
- ½ teaspoon ground black pepper
- 1 cup shredded sharp Cheddar cheese
- 4 slices bacon, cooked and crumbled
- 1 cup panko bread crumbs

1. Preheat the air fryer to 400°F. Cut parchment paper to fit the air fryer basket.
2. In a large bowl, mix mashed potatoes, ½ cup sour cream, salt, pepper, Cheddar, and bacon. Form twelve balls using 2 tablespoons of the potato mixture per ball.
3. Divide remaining ¼ cup sour cream evenly among mashed potato balls, coating each before rolling in bread crumbs.
4. Place balls on parchment in the air fryer basket and spritz with cooking spray. Cook 10 minutes until brown. Serve warm.

PER SERVING

CALORIES: 400 | **FAT:** 24g | **PROTEIN:** 15g | **SODIUM:** 1,290mg | **FIBER:** 0g | **CARBOHYDRATES:** 33g | **SUGAR:** 3g

Foil Packet Lemon Butter Asparagus

Just as they do in the oven, foil packets work like mini steamers in the air fryer too. They allow the vegetables to cook without crisping the edges and also help retain flavor. This dish is deliciously fresh tasting and would go great with the Lemon Butter–Dill Salmon in Chapter 7.

Pantry Staples: salt, ground black pepper
Hands-On Time: 5 minutes
Cook Time: 15 minutes

Serves 4

1 pound asparagus, ends trimmed
¼ cup salted butter, cubed
Zest and juice of ½ medium lemon
½ teaspoon salt
¼ teaspoon ground black pepper

1. Preheat the air fryer to 375°F. Cut a 6" × 6" square of foil.
2. Place asparagus on foil square.
3. Dot asparagus with butter. Sprinkle lemon zest, salt, and pepper on top of asparagus. Drizzle lemon juice over asparagus.
4. Fold foil over asparagus and seal the edges closed to form a packet.
5. Place in the air fryer basket and cook 15 minutes until tender. Serve warm.

PER SERVING

CALORIES: 130 | **FAT:** 12g | **PROTEIN:** 3g | **SODIUM:** 380mg | **FIBER:** 2g | **CARBOHYDRATES:** 5g | **SUGAR:** 2g

Easy Green Bean Casserole

This dish is a classic made easy. Whether you're making it for a gathering or just need an easy weeknight win, this recipe is sure to please. The creamy sauce and crunchy topping make every bite perfection, and you get to enjoy a good serving of vegetables.

Pantry Staples: salt, ground black pepper
Hands-On Time: 10 minutes
Cook Time: 20 minutes

Serves 4

- **1 (10-ounce) can condensed cream of mushroom soup**
- **¼ cup heavy cream**
- **2 (14.5-ounce) cans cut green beans, drained**
- **1 teaspoon minced garlic**
- **½ teaspoon salt**
- **¼ teaspoon ground black pepper**
- **1 cup packaged French fried onions**

1. Preheat the air fryer to 320°F.
2. In a 4-quart baking dish, pour soup and cream over green beans and mix to combine.
3. Stir in garlic, salt, and pepper until combined. Top with French fried onions.
4. Place in the air fryer basket and cook 20 minutes until top is lightly brown and dish is heated through. Serve warm.

PER SERVING

CALORIES: 240 | **FAT:** 17g | **PROTEIN:** 5g | **SODIUM:** 1,420mg | **FIBER:** 4g | **CARBOHYDRATES:** 20g | **SUGAR:** 4g

Yeast Rolls

You might be surprised that you can make bakery-quality rolls in your air fryer. Not only do they cook faster, but you also won't even believe they weren't baked in the oven. These golden-topped rolls are the perfect addition to any meal on any occasion. If you love extra-sweet rolls, try a drizzle of honey butter over the top.

Pantry Staples: granulated sugar, salt, all-purpose flour
Hands-On Time: 10 minutes
Cook Time: 1 hour 10 minutes

Serves 16

4 tablespoons salted butter
¼ cup granulated sugar
1 cup hot water
1 tablespoon quick-rise yeast
1 large egg
1 teaspoon salt
2½ cups all-purpose flour, divided

1. In a microwave-safe bowl, microwave butter 30 seconds until melted. Pour 2 tablespoons of butter into a large bowl. Add sugar, hot water, and yeast. Mix until yeast is dissolved.
2. Using a rubber spatula, mix in egg, salt, and 2¼ cups flour. Dough will be very sticky.
3. Cover bowl with plastic wrap and let rise in a warm place 1 hour.
4. Sprinkle remaining ¼ cup flour on dough and turn onto a lightly floured surface. Knead 2 minutes, then cut into sixteen even pieces.
5. Preheat the air fryer to 350°F. Spray a 6" round cake pan with cooking spray.
6. Sprinkle each roll with flour and arrange in pan. Brush with remaining melted butter. Place pan in the air fryer basket and cook 10 minutes until fluffy and golden on top. Serve warm.

PER SERVING

CALORIES: 110 | **FAT:** 3g | **PROTEIN:** 3g | **SODIUM:** 170mg | **FIBER:** 1g | **CARBOHYDRATES:** 18g | **SUGAR:** 3g

BEST TEMPERATURE FOR RISING DOUGH

To achieve a good rise, yeast usually needs to be in an environment that's around 70°F. This is easy to come by in the summer but can be more difficult in the winter. If your dough isn't rising, warm your oven for 15 minutes on the Warm setting or 200°F, then turn it off. Place your dough in a large, oven-safe bowl and cover with foil. Place into the warmed oven for the length of rising time.

Southwest-Style Corn Cobs

This recipe is a great way to add some variety to your side dishes. Adding cheese with a splash of lime juice can really brighten this vegetable and extend its versatility. This recipe uses cotija cheese, which can often be found near the Mexican cheeses at the grocery store.

Pantry Staples: salt
Hands-On Time: 5 minutes
Cook Time: 15 minutes

Serves 6

- ½ cup sour cream
- 1½ teaspoons chili powder
- Juice and zest of 1 medium lime
- ¼ teaspoon salt
- 6 mini corn cobs
- ½ cup crumbled cotija cheese

1. Preheat the air fryer to 350°F.
2. In a medium bowl, mix sour cream, chili powder, lime zest and juice, and salt.
3. Brush mixture all over corn cobs and place them in the air fryer basket. Cook 15 minutes until corn is tender.
4. Sprinkle with cotija and serve.

PER SERVING

CALORIES: 130 | **FAT:** 6g | **PROTEIN:** 5g | **SODIUM:** 290mg | **FIBER:** 3g | **CARBOHYDRATES:** 12g | **SUGAR:** 4g

Cheesy Garlic Bread

This quick dish is perfect for a side or even a tasty snack. The simple dough gives the cheese bread a little tang, which goes great with the savory garlic-butter flavors. The golden, gooey cheese makes every bite delicious, and it all comes together in less than 30 minutes.

Pantry Staples: none
Hands-On Time: 10 minutes
Cook Time: 12 minutes

Serves 6

- **1 cup self-rising flour**
- **1 cup plain full-fat Greek yogurt**
- **¼ cup salted butter, softened**
- **1 tablespoon minced garlic**
- **1 cup shredded mozzarella cheese**

1. Preheat the air fryer to 320°F. Cut parchment paper to fit the air fryer basket.
2. In a large bowl, mix flour and yogurt until a sticky, soft dough forms. Let sit 5 minutes.
3. Turn dough onto a lightly floured surface. Knead dough 1 minute, then transfer to prepared parchment. Press out into an 8" round.
4. In a small bowl, mix butter and garlic. Brush over dough. Sprinkle with mozzarella.
5. Place in the air fryer and cook 12 minutes until edges are golden and cheese is brown. Serve warm.

PER SERVING

CALORIES: 250 | **FAT:** 14g | **PROTEIN:** 12g | **SODIUM:** 450mg | **FIBER:** 1g | **CARBOHYDRATES:** 18g | **SUGAR:** 2g

Cheddar-Garlic Drop Biscuits

Sometimes you just need an easy side. This recipe is an excellent complement to any comfort-food dinner, from chili to chicken. The crispy golden edges and soft fluffy centers combine for the perfect bite. The cheese adds a flavor that makes this biscuit unforgettable.

Pantry Staples: all-purpose flour, baking powder, salt
Hands-On Time: 5 minutes
Cook Time: 10 minutes per batch

Serves 10

- **2 cups all-purpose flour**
- **1 tablespoon baking powder**
- **1 teaspoon salt**
- **½ teaspoon garlic powder**
- **¾ cup sour cream**
- **¾ cup salted butter, melted, divided**
- **1 cup shredded Cheddar cheese**

1. Preheat the air fryer to 400°F.
2. In a large bowl, mix flour, baking powder, salt, garlic powder, sour cream, and ½ cup butter until well combined. Gently stir in Cheddar.
3. Using your hands, form dough into ten even-sized balls.
4. Place balls in the air fryer basket, working in batches as necessary. Cook 10 minutes until golden and crispy on the edges.
5. Remove biscuits from the air fryer and brush with remaining ¼ cup melted butter to serve.

PER SERVING

CALORIES: 290 | **FAT:** 21g | **PROTEIN:** 6g | **SODIUM:** 330mg | **FIBER:** 1g | **CARBOHYDRATES:** 21g | **SUGAR:** 0g

Tater Tots

This is a dish both kids and adults will love. While store-bought tater tots take less time to make, this three-ingredient recipe will have you wondering why you haven't made them at home before. The fresh taste of the potatoes can't be beat, and the crispy golden edges will keep you reaching for more.

Pantry Staples: salt, ground black pepper
Hands-On Time: 15 minutes
Cook Time: 25 minutes

Serves 4

4 cups water
1 pound russet potatoes, peeled
½ teaspoon salt
½ teaspoon ground black pepper

1. In a large saucepan over medium-high heat, bring the water to a boil. Add potatoes and boil about 10 minutes until a fork can be easily inserted into them. Drain potatoes and let cool.
2. Preheat the air fryer to 350°F.
3. Grate potatoes into a large bowl. Add salt and pepper and mix gently by hand.
4. Form potatoes into sixteen 1-tablespoon tater tot–shaped balls. Place tater tots in the air fryer basket and spray lightly with cooking spray.
5. Cook 15 minutes, shaking the basket halfway through cooking time, until crispy and brown. Serve warm.

PER SERVING

CALORIES: 90 | **FAT:** 0g | **PROTEIN:** 2g | **SODIUM:** 300mg | **FIBER:** 2g | **CARBOHYDRATES:** 20g | **SUGAR:** 1g

Cheesy Cauliflower Tots

Cauliflower-based foods have risen in popularity recently, and for good reason. Cauliflower is a healthy and delicious vegetable that's extremely versatile. It's the perfect substitute for potatoes if you're trying to cut down on the carbs.

Pantry Staples: all-purpose flour, salt, ground black pepper
Hands-On Time: 15 minutes
Cook Time: 12 minutes per batch

Serves 4

- **1 (10-ounce) steamer bag riced cauliflower**
- **⅓ cup Italian bread crumbs**
- **¼ cup all-purpose flour**
- **1 large egg**
- **¾ cup shredded sharp Cheddar cheese**
- **½ teaspoon salt**
- **¼ teaspoon ground black pepper**

1. Cook cauliflower according to the package directions. Let cool, then squeeze in a cheesecloth or kitchen towel to drain excess water.
2. Preheat the air fryer to 400°F. Cut parchment paper to fit the air fryer basket.
3. In a large bowl, mix drained cauliflower, bread crumbs, flour, egg, and Cheddar. Sprinkle in salt and pepper, then mix until well combined.
4. Roll 2 tablespoons of mixture into a tot shape. Repeat to use all of the mixture.
5. Place tots on parchment in the air fryer basket, working in batches as necessary. Spritz with cooking spray. Cook 12 minutes, turning tots halfway through cooking time, until golden brown. Serve warm.

PER SERVING

CALORIES: 180 | **FAT:** 8g | **PROTEIN:** 10g | **SODIUM:** 600mg | **FIBER:** 0g | **CARBOHYDRATES:** 17g | **SUGAR:** 2g

Zucchini Fries

The secret to these flavorful fries is to remove as much moisture as possible before cooking them. This makes for a tasty crunch and perfectly dippable fries. When choosing zucchini for this recipe, make sure you get ones that are firm and just ripe, because if they start out too soft, you'll likely end up with soggy fries.

Pantry Staples: salt
Hands-On Time: 10 minutes
Cook Time: 42 minutes

Serves 4

3 large zucchini, trimmed
2 teaspoons salt
2 large eggs, whisked
1 cup grated Parmesan cheese
1 cup panko bread crumbs
2 teaspoons Italian seasoning

1. Cut a zucchini in half crosswise. Slice down the length of each half, then cut each new piece in half lengthwise, to make eight sticks. Repeat with remaining zucchini for a total of twenty-four sticks.
2. Spread zucchini fries in a single layer on top of a paper towel and sprinkle with salt. The salt will help draw out excess moisture. Place more paper towels on top of zucchini fries to absorb moisture. Let sit 30 minutes, changing paper towels out halfway through time.
3. Preheat the air fryer to 400°F.
4. Place eggs in a medium bowl. Place Parmesan, bread crumbs, and Italian seasoning in a zippered storage bag. Dip six fries into egg, then place into storage bag and shake to coat. Remove and repeat with remaining zucchini.
5. Spritz fries with cooking spray and place in the air fryer basket, working in batches as necessary.
6. Cook 12 minutes, turning halfway through cooking time, until crisp and brown. Serve warm.

PER SERVING

CALORIES: 280 | **FAT:** 11g | **PROTEIN:** 16g | **SODIUM:** 1,800mg | **FIBER:** 2g | **CARBOHYDRATES:** 30g | **SUGAR:** 7g

5

Chicken Main Dishes

Chicken is an extremely popular protein, and for good reasons—it's inexpensive, quick to make, and delicious. But your chicken dinner routine can get boring fast! And you can quickly grow as tired of making it as you are of eating it.

The good news is your air fryer can cook up juicy chicken, bursting with flavor, in practically no time at all. And this chapter is full of innovative recipes to change up your chicken routine, from Chicken Parmesan Casserole to Buffalo Chicken Sandwiches!

15-Minute Chicken

Chicken is such a versatile ingredient that it's important to have a base recipe for preparing it in a delicious way. This recipe can be served as your main entrée or transformed into countless dinners by way of leftovers. It also provides the perfect seasoning for that classic chicken flavor that you love.

Pantry Staples: salt, ground black pepper
Hands-On Time: 7 minutes
Cook Time: 15 minutes

Serves 4

4 (6-ounce) boneless, skinless chicken breasts
2 tablespoons olive oil
1 teaspoon salt
1 teaspoon garlic powder
1 teaspoon paprika
½ teaspoon ground black pepper

SAVING TIME

For busy families, saving time in the kitchen can be very important. This chicken recipe can be used in recipes in this chapter like Chicken-Cream Cheese Taquitos or Baked Chicken Nachos. It's a great recipe to make at the beginning of a week so you can use it in any recipe you might need later on to cut down your active cooking time.

1. Preheat the air fryer to 375°F.
2. Carefully butterfly chicken breasts lengthwise, leaving the two halves connected. Drizzle chicken with oil, then sprinkle with salt, garlic powder, paprika, and pepper.
3. Place in the air fryer basket and cook 15 minutes, turning halfway through cooking time, until chicken is golden brown and the internal temperature reaches at least 165°F. Serve warm.

PER SERVING

CALORIES: 270 | **FAT:** 11g | **PROTEIN:** 39g | **SODIUM:** 660mg | **FIBER:** 0g | **CARBOHYDRATES:** 1g | **SUGAR:** 0g

Baked Chicken Nachos

Whether it's game day or just a weeknight in need of an easy meal, this recipe will elevate your nacho game. Layering the nachos lets you have all the topping flavors in every bite. This is a great way to use up leftover chicken and make it into a whole new meal.

Pantry Staples: none
Hands-On Time: 5 minutes
Cook Time: 7 minutes

Serves 4

50 tortilla chips
2 cups shredded cooked chicken breast, divided
2 cups shredded Mexican-blend cheese, divided
½ cup sliced pickled jalapeño peppers, divided
½ cup diced red onion, divided

1. Preheat the air fryer to 300°F.
2. Use foil to make a bowl shape that fits the shape of the air fryer basket. Place half tortilla chips in the bottom of foil bowl, then top with 1 cup chicken, 1 cup cheese, ¼ cup jalapeños, and ¼ cup onion. Repeat with remaining chips and toppings.
3. Place foil bowl in the air fryer basket and cook 7 minutes until cheese is melted and toppings heated through. Serve warm.

PER SERVING

CALORIES: 460 | **FAT:** 25g | **PROTEIN:** 32g | **SODIUM:** 430mg | **FIBER:** 1g | **CARBOHYDRATES:** 25g | **SUGAR:** 2g

CUSTOMIZE IT

Feel free to add your favorite toppings to make this dish your own. Diced tomatoes, shredded lettuce, salsa, and sour cream are all great additions to this quick and easy meal.

Pretzel-Crusted Chicken

The saltiness of pretzels makes them one of the most popular snack foods around, but did you know that grinding them up also makes for the perfect breading? This Pretzel-Crusted Chicken is the perfect way to change up your weeknight chicken menu, especially when you serve it with different dipping sauces.

Pantry Staples: salt, ground black pepper
Hands-On Time: 10 minutes
Cook Time: 12 minutes

Serves 4

- 2 cups mini twist pretzels
- ½ cup mayonnaise
- 2 tablespoons honey
- 2 tablespoons yellow mustard
- 4 (6-ounce) boneless, skinless chicken breasts, sliced in half lengthwise
- 1 teaspoon salt
- ½ teaspoon ground black pepper

1. Preheat the air fryer to 375°F.
2. In a food processor, place pretzels and pulse ten times.
3. In a medium bowl, mix mayonnaise, honey, and mustard.
4. Sprinkle chicken with salt and pepper, then brush with sauce mixture until well coated.
5. Pour pretzel crumbs onto a shallow plate and press each piece of chicken into them until well coated.
6. Spritz chicken with cooking spray and place in the air fryer basket. Cook 12 minutes, turning halfway through cooking time, until edges are golden brown and the internal temperature reaches at least 165°F. Serve warm.

PER SERVING

CALORIES: 520 | **FAT:** 28g | **PROTEIN:** 40g | **SODIUM:** 1,330mg | **FIBER:** 1g | **CARBOHYDRATES:** 40g | **SUGAR:** 10g

Parmesan Chicken Tenders

This meal is perfect for weeknights. In less than 30 minutes, you can be enjoying a delicious dinner. This dish is perfect for adults and kids alike, as the flavors are mild and can be tailored to your taste by adding your favorite dipping sauce, such as marinara, ranch, or even ketchup.

Pantry Staples: salt, ground black pepper
Hands-On Time: 10 minutes
Cook Time: 12 minutes

Serves 4

1 pound boneless, skinless chicken breast tenderloins
½ cup mayonnaise
1 cup grated Parmesan cheese
1 cup panko bread crumbs
½ teaspoon garlic powder
1 teaspoon salt
½ teaspoon ground black pepper

1. Preheat the air fryer to 400°F.
2. In a large bowl, add chicken and mayonnaise and toss to coat.
3. In a medium bowl, mix Parmesan, bread crumbs, garlic powder, salt, and pepper. Press chicken into bread crumb mixture to fully coat. Spritz with cooking spray and place in the air fryer basket.
4. Cook 12 minutes, turning halfway through cooking time, until tenders are golden and crisp on the edges and internal temperature reaches at least 165°F. Serve warm.

PER SERVING

CALORIES: 460 | **FAT:** 28g | **PROTEIN:** 34g | **SODIUM:** 1,220mg | **FIBER:** 0g | **CARBOHYDRATES:** 18g | **SUGAR:** 1g

Crispy Cajun Fried Chicken

Fried chicken doesn't have to be intimidating. Thanks to your air fryer, you can achieve a wonderful flavor and texture in a healthier way. Instead of loads of vegetable oil, the secret to the crispy exterior in this recipe is cooking spray spritzed onto the flour the chicken is dredged in. Do not skip this step, as it helps the exterior brown and crisp up in a delicious way.

Pantry Staples: all-purpose flour
Hands-On Time: 15 minutes
Cook Time: 50 minutes

Serves 4

4 (6-ounce) boneless, skinless chicken thighs
¾ cup buttermilk
⅓ cup hot sauce
1½ tablespoons Cajun seasoning, divided
1 cup all-purpose flour
1 large egg

1. Preheat the air fryer to 375°F.
2. In a large bowl, combine chicken thighs, buttermilk, hot sauce, and ½ tablespoon Cajun seasoning, and toss to coat. Cover and let marinate in refrigerator at least 30 minutes.
3. In a large bowl, whisk flour with ½ tablespoon Cajun seasoning. In a medium bowl, whisk egg.
4. Remove chicken from marinade and sprinkle with remaining ½ tablespoon Cajun seasoning.
5. Dredge chicken by dipping into egg, then pressing into flour to fully coat. Spritz with cooking spray and place into the air fryer basket.
6. Cook 20 minutes, turning halfway through cooking time, until chicken is golden brown and internal temperature reaches at least 165°F. Serve warm.

PER SERVING

CALORIES: 340 | **FAT:** 8g | **PROTEIN:** 39g | **SODIUM:** 700mg | **FIBER:** 1g | **CARBOHYDRATES:** 26g | **SUGAR:** 0g

Buffalo Chicken Sandwiches

This quick meal isn't short on flavor. The crispy chicken paired with the tangy sauce makes a delicious meal even without breading. Feel free to add lettuce and tomato for a deluxe version.

Pantry Staples: none
Hands-On Time: 15 minutes
Cook Time: 20 minutes

Serves 4

- 4 (6-ounce) boneless, skinless chicken thighs
- 1 (1-ounce) packet dry ranch seasoning
- ¼ cup buffalo sauce
- 4 (1-ounce) slices pepper jack cheese
- 4 sandwich buns

1. Preheat the air fryer to 375°F.
2. Sprinkle each chicken thigh with ranch seasoning and spritz with cooking spray.
3. Place chicken in the air fryer basket and cook 20 minutes, turning chicken halfway through, until chicken is brown at the edges and internal temperature reaches at least 165°F.
4. Drizzle buffalo sauce over chicken, top with a slice of cheese, and place on buns to serve.

PER SERVING

CALORIES: 480 | **FAT:** 20g | **PROTEIN:** 47g | **SODIUM:** 1,300mg | **FIBER:** 0g | **CARBOHYDRATES:** 23g | **SUGAR:** 3g

Zesty Ranch Chicken Drumsticks

Drumsticks are a convenient cut of meat that is perfect for weeknight dinners. Not only are drumsticks budget-friendly, but they also have a ton of flavor. Pair this meal with Roasted Broccoli or Potato Wedges (see both recipes in Chapter 4) for a complete meal.

Pantry Staples: salt, ground black pepper
Hands-On Time: 10 minutes
Cook Time: 20 minutes

Serves 4

- 8 (4-ounce) chicken drumsticks
- 1 teaspoon salt
- ½ teaspoon ground black pepper
- ¼ cup dry ranch seasoning
- ½ cup panko bread crumbs
- ½ cup grated Parmesan cheese

1. Preheat the air fryer to 375°F.
2. Sprinkle drumsticks with salt, pepper, and ranch seasoning.
3. In a paper lunch bag, combine bread crumbs and Parmesan. Add drumsticks to the bag and shake to coat. Spritz with cooking spray.
4. Place drumsticks in the air fryer basket and cook 20 minutes, turning halfway through cooking time, until the internal temperature reaches at least 165°F. Serve warm.

PER SERVING

CALORIES: 250 | **FAT:** 8g | **PROTEIN:** 29g | **SODIUM:** 1,600mg | **FIBER:** 0g | **CARBOHYDRATES:** 9g | **SUGAR:** 0g

Barbecue Chicken Enchiladas

Here's a fun and flavorful spin on a Mexican-inspired classic. Switching up the flavor profile of classic enchiladas makes for a sweet and savory dish you won't be able to put down. Sweet barbecue sauce covers the dish and makes every bite melt-in-your-mouth delicious. The cheesy inside gets the perfect bit of crunch from the onion. This meal would be perfect with leftover grilled chicken.

Pantry Staples: none
Hands-On Time: 10 minutes
Cook Time: 15 minutes per batch

Serves 4

- **1½ cups barbecue sauce, divided**
- **3 cups shredded cooked chicken**
- **8 (6") flour tortillas**
- **1½ cups shredded Mexican-blend cheese, divided**
- **⅓ cup diced red onion**

1. Preheat the air fryer to 350°F.
2. In a large bowl, mix 1 cup barbecue sauce and shredded chicken.
3. Place ¼ cup chicken onto each tortilla and top with 2 tablespoons cheese.
4. Roll each tortilla and place seam side down into two 6" round baking dishes. Brush tortillas with remaining sauce, top with remaining cheese, and sprinkle with onion.
5. Working in batches, place in the air fryer basket and cook 15 minutes until the sauce is bubbling and cheese is melted. Serve warm.

PER SERVING

CALORIES: 640 | **FAT:** 19g | **PROTEIN:** 41g | **SODIUM:** 1,850mg | **FIBER:** 0g | **CARBOHYDRATES:** 76g | **SUGAR:** 37g

Chicken–Cream Cheese Taquitos

In less than 15 minutes you can enjoy this flavorful dish. It's simple but will still be a huge hit with the family. Either leftover cooked chicken or shredded rotisserie chicken from the store will be perfect in this recipe. Try serving with a variety of dipping sauces, such as salsa, sour cream, and guacamole, for a tasty meal that everyone can enjoy.

Pantry Staples: none
Hands-On Time: 5 minutes
Cook Time: 8 minutes

Serves 4

- **1½ cups shredded cooked chicken**
- **4 ounces full-fat cream cheese, softened**
- **1 cup shredded sharp Cheddar cheese**
- **12 (6") white corn tortillas**

1. Preheat the air fryer to 350°F.
2. In a large bowl, mix chicken, cream cheese, and Cheddar.
3. Place 3 tablespoons chicken mixture onto each tortilla and roll. Spritz each roll with cooking spray.
4. Place seam side down in the air fryer basket and cook 8 minutes, turning halfway through cooking time, until crispy and brown. Serve warm.

PER SERVING

CALORIES: 430 | **FAT:** 21g | **PROTEIN:** 24g | **SODIUM:** 320mg | **FIBER:** 0g | **CARBOHYDRATES:** 37g | **SUGAR:** 4g

Teriyaki Chicken Kebabs

This flavorful meal is great for meal prepping but fast enough to make any night of the week. Try adding a side of rice to make this meal even more filling. Reheat the leftovers 5 minutes in the air fryer at 280°F.

Pantry Staples: salt, ground black pepper
Hands-On Time: 10 minutes
Cook Time: 1 hour 15 minutes

Serves 4

- **¾ cup teriyaki sauce, divided**
- **4 (4-ounce) boneless, skinless chicken thighs, cubed**
- **1 teaspoon salt**
- **½ teaspoon ground black pepper**
- **1 cup pineapple chunks**
- **1 medium red bell pepper, seeded and cut into 1" cubes**
- **¼ medium yellow onion, peeled and cut into 1" cubes**

1. In a large bowl, pour ½ cup teriyaki sauce over chicken and sprinkle with salt and black pepper. Cover and let marinate in refrigerator 1 hour.
2. Soak eight 6" skewers in water at least 10 minutes to prevent burning. Preheat the air fryer to 400°F.
3. Place a cube of chicken on skewer, then a piece of pineapple, bell pepper, and onion. Repeat with remaining chicken, pineapple, and vegetables.
4. Brush kebabs with remaining ¼ cup teriyaki sauce and place in the air fryer basket. Cook 15 minutes, turning twice during cooking, until chicken reaches an internal temperature of at least 165°F and vegetables are tender. Serve warm.

PER SERVING

CALORIES: 190 | **FAT:** 4.5g | **PROTEIN:** 25g | **SODIUM:** 630mg | **FIBER:** 1g | **CARBOHYDRATES:** 13g | **SUGAR:** 9g

Buttermilk-Fried Chicken Thighs

Buttermilk is a tangy ingredient that will take your fried chicken to the next level and give it a true southern taste. When combined with the flavorful and fatty chicken thighs, it's nothing short of perfection. If you don't have buttermilk on hand, you can easily make your own substitute by combining 1 tablespoon white vinegar with 1 cup milk.

Pantry Staples: all-purpose flour
Hands-On Time: 15 minutes
Cook Time: 1 hour

Serves 4

- **1 cup buttermilk**
- **2 tablespoons seasoned salt, divided**
- **1 pound bone-in, skin-on chicken thighs**
- **1 cup all-purpose flour**
- **¼ cup cornstarch**

COOKING SPRAY IS ESSENTIAL

Spraying your chicken before, and sometimes during, cooking helps it to crisp up and get that amazing golden brown color. Failure to do so will result in a very dry, floury-tasting end result.

1. In a large bowl, combine buttermilk and 1 tablespoon seasoned salt. Add chicken. Cover and let marinate in refrigerator 30 minutes.
2. Preheat the air fryer to 375°F.
3. In a separate bowl, mix flour, cornstarch, and remaining seasoned salt. Dredge chicken thighs, one at a time, in flour mixture, covering completely.
4. Spray chicken generously with cooking spray, being sure that no dry spots remain. Place chicken in the air fryer basket and cook 30 minutes, turning halfway through cooking time and spraying any dry spots, until chicken is dark golden brown and crispy and internal temperature reaches at least 165°F.
5. Serve warm.

PER SERVING

CALORIES: 230 | **FAT:** 3g | **PROTEIN:** 17g | **SODIUM:** 1,130mg | **FIBER:** 1g | **CARBOHYDRATES:** 32g | **SUGAR:** 0g

Jerk Chicken Wings

Jamaican jerk chicken is an authentic Caribbean favorite with savory flavor and plenty of spice. The main ingredient in this recipe is the jerk chicken seasoning. For the best flavor, you'll want a traditional blend that uses Scotch bonnet peppers. Walkerswood is an excellent brand for traditional flavor and can be found at most grocery stores.

Pantry Staples: salt
Hands-On Time: 5 minutes
Cook Time: 1 hour 20 minutes

Serves 4

- **¼ cup Jamaican jerk marinade**
- **1 teaspoon onion powder**
- **1 teaspoon garlic powder**
- **1 teaspoon salt**
- **2 pounds chicken wings, flats and drums separated**

1. In a large bowl, combine jerk seasoning, onion powder, garlic powder, and salt. Add chicken wings and toss to coat well. Cover and let marinate in refrigerator at least 1 hour.
2. Preheat the air fryer to 400°F.
3. Place wings in the air fryer basket in a single layer, working in batches as necessary. Cook wings 20 minutes, turning halfway through cooking time, until internal temperature reaches at least 165°F. Cool 5 minutes before serving.

PER SERVING

CALORIES: 230 | **FAT:** 16g | **PROTEIN:** 21g | **SODIUM:** 250mg | **FIBER:** 21g | **CARBOHYDRATES:** 1g | **SUGAR:** 0g

Chicken Cordon Bleu

Chicken dinners can sometimes feel monotonous, but this crunchy classic is anything but boring. In 30 minutes, you can make this family favorite with even more crunch than the oven alone can offer. The inside is filled with gooey melted cheese that makes every bite perfect.

Pantry Staples: salt, ground black pepper
Hands-On Time: 15 minutes
Cook Time: 15 minutes

Serves 4

- **4 (6-ounce) boneless, skinless chicken breasts**
- **¾ teaspoon salt**
- **½ teaspoon ground black pepper**
- **8 (2.25-ounce) slices deli Black Forest ham**
- **8 (1-ounce) slices Gruyère cheese**
- **1 large egg, beaten**
- **2 cups panko bread crumbs**

1. Preheat the air fryer to 375°F.
2. Cut each chicken breast in half lengthwise. Use a mallet to pound to ¼" thickness. Sprinkle salt and pepper on each side of chicken.
3. Place a slice of ham and a slice of cheese on each piece of chicken. Roll up chicken and secure with toothpicks.
4. In a medium bowl, add egg. In a separate medium bowl, add bread crumbs. Dip each chicken roll into egg, then into bread crumbs, pressing gently to adhere.
5. Spritz rolls with cooking spray and place in the air fryer basket. Cook 15 minutes, turning halfway through cooking time, until rolls are golden brown and internal temperature reaches at least 165°F. Serve warm.

PER SERVING

CALORIES: 710 | **FAT:** 27g | **PROTEIN:** 81g | **SODIUM:** 2,250mg | **FIBER:** 0g | **CARBOHYDRATES:** 30g | **SUGAR:** 1g

Dill Pickle–Ranch Wings

Pickles have a unique flavor that makes them easy to love. This recipe puts the pickle juice to good use in a marinade. The dill flavor with a zesty kick of vinegar makes these wings stand out.

Pantry Staples: salt, ground black pepper
Hands-On Time: 5 minutes
Cook Time: 2 hours 20 minutes

Serves 4

- **1 cup pickle juice**
- **2 pounds chicken wings, flats and drums separated**
- **½ teaspoon salt**
- **½ teaspoon ground black pepper**
- **2 teaspoons dry ranch seasoning**

MARINATING TIME
To achieve the best pickle flavor, these wings are marinated for 2 hours, but if you're short on time you can marinate them for as little as 30 minutes. They won't have the same deep flavor, but you'll still get to enjoy a tangy dill crunch.

1. In a large bowl or resealable plastic bag, combine pickle juice and wings. Cover and let marinate in refrigerator 2 hours.
2. Preheat the air fryer to 400°F.
3. In a separate bowl, mix salt, pepper, and ranch seasoning. Remove wings from marinade and toss in dry seasoning.
4. Place wings in the air fryer basket in a single layer, working in batches as necessary. Cook 20 minutes, turning halfway through cooking time, until wings reach an internal temperature of at least 165°F. Cool 5 minutes before serving.

PER SERVING

CALORIES: 240 | **FAT:** 16g | **PROTEIN:** 21g | **SODIUM:** 510mg | **FIBER:** 0g | **CARBOHYDRATES:** 0g | **SUGAR:** 0g

Buffalo Chicken Meatballs

Buffalo sauce is the perfect flavor for game day gatherings because it's available in a variety of spice levels for everyone to enjoy. These meatballs are packed with flavor and can even be made ahead of time because they reheat so well. Because chicken can easily dry out, these meatballs use mayonnaise as a binder instead of eggs. The higher fat content keeps them juicy while adding even more flavor.

Pantry Staples: none
Hands-On Time: 10 minutes
Cook Time: 12 minutes

Serves 5

- **1 pound ground chicken breast**
- **1 (1-ounce) packet dry ranch seasoning**
- **⅓ cup plain bread crumbs**
- **3 tablespoons mayonnaise**
- **5 tablespoons buffalo sauce, divided**

MAKE IT A MEAL

Try placing a few meatballs on a 6" sub roll and top with blue cheese to make a delicious and tangy sandwich.

1. Preheat the air fryer to 370°F.
2. In a large bowl, mix chicken, ranch seasoning, bread crumbs, and mayonnaise. Pour in 2 tablespoons buffalo sauce and stir to combine.
3. Roll meat mixture into balls, about 2 tablespoons for each, to make twenty meatballs.
4. Place meatballs in the air fryer basket and cook 12 minutes, shaking the basket twice during cooking, until brown and internal temperature reaches at least 165°F.
5. Toss meatballs in remaining buffalo sauce and serve.

PER SERVING (SERVING SIZE: 4 MEATBALLS)

CALORIES: 240 | **FAT:** 12g | **PROTEIN:** 22g | **SODIUM:** 22mg | **FIBER:** 0g | **CARBOHYDRATES:** 6g | **SUGAR:** 1g

Blackened Chicken Tenders

Blackened seasoning refers to a technique that coats the meat in a variety of delicious and aromatic herbs that give it a darkened appearance when cooked. These herbs are similar to Cajun-style seasonings but are often less spicy. This recipe makes a quick homemade seasoning that will give your chicken a dark brown appearance and out-of-this-world flavor. These tenders taste great served with ranch dressing for dipping.

Pantry Staples: salt, ground black pepper
Hands-On Time: 10 minutes
Cook Time: 12 minutes

Serves 4

1 pound boneless, skinless chicken tenders
2 teaspoons paprika
1 teaspoon garlic powder
1 teaspoon salt
½ teaspoon cayenne pepper
½ teaspoon dried thyme
½ teaspoon ground black pepper

1. Preheat the air fryer to 400°F.
2. Place chicken tenders into a large bowl.
3. In a small bowl, mix paprika, garlic powder, salt, cayenne, thyme, and black pepper. Add spice mixture to chicken and toss to coat. Spritz chicken with cooking spray.
4. Place chicken in the air fryer basket and cook 12 minutes, turning halfway through cooking time, until chicken is brown at the edges and internal temperature reaches at least 165°F. Serve warm.

PER SERVING

CALORIES: 130 | **FAT:** 1.5g | **PROTEIN:** 26g | **SODIUM:** 660mg | **FIBER:** 1g | **CARBOHYDRATES:** 2g | **SUGAR:** 0g

Chicken Parmesan Casserole

This savory dish is surprisingly simple and needs only 10 minutes of prep time. It requires precooked chicken, which is perfect if you have leftovers. You can also make it using 15-Minute Chicken (see recipe in this chapter). If you love lots of marinara sauce and gooey bubbling cheese, this mouthwatering dish has everything you need.

Pantry Staples: salt, ground black pepper
Hands-On Time: 10 minutes
Cook Time: 20 minutes

Serves 4

- 2 cups cubed cooked chicken breast
- ½ teaspoon salt
- ¼ teaspoon ground black pepper
- ¾ cup marinara sauce
- 2 teaspoons Italian seasoning, divided
- 1 cup shredded mozzarella cheese
- ½ cup grated Parmesan cheese

1. Preheat the air fryer to 320°F.
2. In a large bowl, toss chicken with salt, pepper, marinara, and 1 teaspoon Italian seasoning.
3. Scrape mixture into a 6" round baking dish. Top with mozzarella, Parmesan, and remaining 1 teaspoon Italian seasoning.
4. Place in the air fryer basket and cook 20 minutes until the sauce is bubbling and cheese is brown and melted. Serve warm.

PER SERVING

CALORIES: 250 | **FAT:** 12g | **PROTEIN:** 32g | **SODIUM:** 900mg | **FIBER:** 0g | **CARBOHYDRATES:** 6g | **SUGAR:** 2g

Barbecue Chicken Drumsticks

This family favorite is perfect for your air fryer. Typically, in the oven you may need to broil your chicken to caramelize the sauce but in the air fryer you get that beautiful dark brown glistening glaze with no extra effort. Try pairing this dish with a side of Macaroni and Cheese from Chapter 4.

Pantry Staples: salt, ground black pepper
Hands-On Time: 5 minutes
Cook Time: 25 minutes

Serves 4

1 teaspoon salt
1 teaspoon chili powder
1 teaspoon garlic powder
½ teaspoon ground black pepper
½ teaspoon onion powder
8 (4-ounce) chicken drumsticks
1 cup barbecue sauce, divided

1. Preheat the air fryer to 375°F.
2. In a large bowl, combine salt, chili powder, garlic powder, pepper, and onion powder. Add drumsticks and toss to fully coat.
3. Brush drumsticks with ¾ cup barbecue sauce to coat.
4. Place in the air fryer basket and cook 25 minutes, turning three times during cooking, until drumsticks are brown and internal temperature reaches at least 165°F.
5. Before serving, brush remaining ¼ cup barbecue sauce over drumsticks. Serve warm.

PER SERVING

CALORIES: 280 | **FAT:** 5g | **PROTEIN:** 26g | **SODIUM:** 1,460mg | **FIBER:** 0g | **CARBOHYDRATES:** 29g | **SUGAR:** 23g

Popcorn Chicken

This is a perfectly poppable dish that will be a favorite among kids and adults alike. The bite-sized breaded chicken is an excellent entrée, or you can mix it into your next crispy chicken salad.

Pantry Staples: salt, ground black pepper
Hands-On Time: 10 minutes
Cook Time: 12 minutes

Serves 4

- 1½ teaspoons salt, divided
- 1 teaspoon ground black pepper, divided
- 1½ teaspoons garlic powder, divided
- 1 tablespoon mayonnaise
- 1 pound boneless, skinless chicken breast, cut into 1" cubes
- 1 cup panko bread crumbs

1. Preheat the air fryer to 350°F.
2. In a large bowl, combine 1 teaspoon salt, ½ teaspoon pepper, 1 teaspoon garlic powder, and mayonnaise. Add chicken cubes and toss to coat.
3. Place bread crumbs in a large resealable bag and add remaining ½ teaspoon salt, ½ teaspoon pepper, and ½ teaspoon garlic powder. Place chicken into the bag and toss to evenly coat.
4. Spritz chicken with cooking spray and place in the air fryer basket. Cook 12 minutes, turning halfway through cooking time, until chicken is golden brown and internal temperature reaches at least 165°F. Serve warm.

PER SERVING

CALORIES: 240 | **FAT:** 6g | **PROTEIN:** 28g | **SODIUM:** 980mg | **FIBER:** 0g | **CARBOHYDRATES:** 16g | **SUGAR:** 1g

Cheesy Chicken and Broccoli Casserole

You may have heard that if you can cook it in the oven, you can cook it in the air fryer—it's true! Even casseroles are great for the air fryer. This dish uses instant rice to make this meal even easier. No separate boiling is needed—the rice cooks right in the dish, soaking up all the delicious flavors of the chicken.

Pantry Staples: salt, ground black pepper
Hands-On Time: 10 minutes
Cook Time: 30 minutes

Serves 4

- **1 pound boneless, skinless chicken breast, cubed**
- **1 teaspoon salt**
- **½ teaspoon ground black pepper**
- **1 cup uncooked instant long-grain white rice**
- **1 cup chopped broccoli florets**
- **1 cup chicken broth**
- **1 cup shredded sharp Cheddar cheese**

1. Preheat the air fryer to 400°F.
2. In a 6" round baking dish, add chicken and sprinkle with salt and pepper.
3. Place in the air fryer basket and cook 10 minutes, stirring twice during cooking.
4. Add rice, broccoli, broth, and Cheddar. Stir until combined. Cover with foil, being sure to tuck foil under the bottom of the dish to ensure the air fryer fan does not blow it off.
5. Place dish back in the air fryer basket and cook 20 minutes until rice is tender. Serve warm.

PER SERVING

CALORIES: 410 | **FAT:** 12g | **PROTEIN:** 36g | **SODIUM:** 1,060mg | **FIBER:** 0g | **CARBOHYDRATES:** 37g | **SUGAR:** 36g

Breaded Chicken Patties

These crispy chicken patties can make for a super-quick and easy homemade sandwich. They're flaky on the outside and cheesy on the inside, giving each bite lots of flavor. To reheat leftovers just pop them in the air fryer at 250°F for 10 minutes.

Pantry Staples: salt, ground black pepper
Hands-On Time: 10 minutes
Cook Time: 15 minutes

Serves 4

1 pound ground chicken breast
1 cup shredded sharp Cheddar cheese
½ cup plain bread crumbs
1 teaspoon salt
½ teaspoon ground black pepper
2 tablespoons mayonnaise
1 cup panko bread crumbs

1. Preheat the air fryer to 400°F.
2. In a large bowl, mix chicken, Cheddar, plain bread crumbs, salt, and pepper until well combined. Separate into four portions and form into patties ½" thick.
3. Brush each patty with mayonnaise, then press into panko bread crumbs to fully coat. Spritz with cooking spray.
4. Place in the air fryer basket and cook 15 minutes, turning halfway through cooking time, until patties are golden brown and internal temperature reaches at least 165°F. Serve warm.

PER SERVING

CALORIES: 400 | **FAT:** 16g | **PROTEIN:** 37g | **SODIUM:** 1,010mg | **FIBER:** 0g | **CARBOHYDRATES:** 26g | **SUGAR:** 1g

GROUND CHICKEN

Ground chicken is increasing in popularity and becoming easily available. You can usually find it in a roll or fresh pack next to the fresh chicken at the grocery store. For this recipe you can also use ground chicken thigh for even more flavor, but it may be more difficult to find.

Chicken Nuggets

Get ready for a kid-friendly dish that's loads better than its fast-food counterpart. These homemade Chicken Nuggets are a breeze to put together, and by using only a few simple ingredients, you'll know exactly what's in your meal.

Pantry Staples: salt, ground black pepper
Hands-On Time: 15 minutes
Cook Time: 10 minutes

Serves 4

1 pound ground chicken breast
1½ teaspoons salt, divided
¾ teaspoon ground black pepper, divided
1½ cups plain bread crumbs, divided
2 large eggs

1. Preheat the air fryer to 400°F.
2. In a large bowl, mix chicken, 1 teaspoon salt, ½ teaspoon pepper, and ½ cup bread crumbs.
3. In a small bowl, whisk eggs. In a separate medium bowl, mix remaining 1 cup bread crumbs with remaining ½ teaspoon salt and ¼ teaspoon pepper.
4. Scoop 1 tablespoon chicken mixture and flatten it into a nugget shape.
5. Dip into eggs, shaking off excess before rolling in bread crumb mixture. Repeat with remaining chicken mixture to make twenty nuggets.
6. Place nuggets in the air fryer basket and spritz with cooking spray. Cook 10 minutes, turning halfway through cooking time, until internal temperature reaches 165°F. Serve warm.

PER SERVING

CALORIES: 360 | **FAT:** 14g | **PROTEIN:** 29g | **SODIUM:** 1,280mg | **FIBER:** 0g | **CARBOHYDRATES:** 29g | **SUGAR:** 2g

Crispy Italian Chicken Thighs

This meal is budget-friendly and loaded with flavor. The super-crispy golden skin gives this meal the perfect crunch.

Pantry Staples: salt, ground black pepper
Hands-On Time: 10 minutes
Cook Time: 25 minutes

Serves 4

½ cup mayonnaise
4 bone-in, skin-on chicken thighs
1 teaspoon salt
½ teaspoon ground black pepper
2 teaspoons Italian seasoning
1 cup Italian bread crumbs

1. Preheat the air fryer to 370°F.
2. Brush mayonnaise over chicken thighs on both sides.
3. Sprinkle thighs with salt, pepper, and Italian seasoning.
4. Place bread crumbs into a resealable plastic bag and add thighs. Shake to coat.
5. Remove thighs from bag and spritz with cooking spray. Place in the air fryer basket and cook 25 minutes, turning thighs after 15 minutes, until skin is golden and crispy and internal temperature reaches at least 165°F.
6. Serve warm.

PER SERVING

CALORIES: 410 | **FAT:** 26g | **PROTEIN:** 24g | **SODIUM:** 1,270mg | **FIBER:** 0g | **CARBOHYDRATES:** 19g | **SUGAR:** 2g

6

Beef and Pork Main Dishes

Beef and pork both offer a solid variety of cuts while remaining relatively inexpensive. Plus, they're both great sources of flavorful protein. Even with all the options, beef and pork can still get boring. This chapter is here to help with exciting ideas that are easy to make and delectable for even the pickiest eaters. From juicy Meatloaf to Calzones bursting with flavor, these recipes give you plenty of amazing beef and pork meals to add to your dinner menu.

Sweet and Spicy Pork Ribs

When it comes to tasty barbecue, it's hard to beat ribs. With your air fryer, you can recreate that perfect summertime flavor without ever firing up the grill. Add your favorite sauce to this easy dry rub to make the flavors sing.

Pantry Staples: salt, ground black pepper
Hands-On Time: 10 minutes
Cook Time: 20 minutes per batch

Serves 4

- **1 (2-pound) rack pork spareribs, white membrane removed**
- **¼ cup brown sugar**
- **2 teaspoons salt**
- **2 teaspoons ground black pepper**
- **1 tablespoon chili powder**
- **1 teaspoon garlic powder**
- **½ teaspoon cayenne pepper**

1. Preheat the air fryer to 400°F.
2. Place ribs on a work surface and cut the rack into two pieces to fit in the air fryer basket.
3. In a medium bowl, whisk together brown sugar, salt, black pepper, chili powder, garlic powder, and cayenne to make a dry rub.
4. Massage dry rub onto both sides of ribs until well coated. Place a portion of ribs in the air fryer basket, working in batches as necessary.
5. Cook 20 minutes until internal temperature reaches at least 190°F and no pink remains. Let rest 5 minutes before cutting and serving.

PER SERVING

CALORIES: 500 | **FAT:** 38g | **PROTEIN:** 25g | **SODIUM:** 1,380mg | **FIBER:** 1g | **CARBOHYDRATES:** 15g | **SUGAR:** 13g

INTERNAL TEMPERATURE

Pork needs to be cooked to an internal temperature of at least 145°F to be considered done. For ribs, this book recommends 190°F because at a higher internal temperature, more of the protein breaks down and softens the meat, making it much easier to pull off the bone.

Honey-Sriracha Pork Ribs

If you love sweet and spicy ribs, this recipe is for you. These ribs are sticky, juicy, and delicious. They're a great alternative to barbecue ribs when you want to change things up but still enjoy lots of flavor in every bite.

Pantry Staples: salt, ground black pepper

Hands-On Time: 10 minutes

Cook Time: 25 minutes

Serves 4

3 pounds pork back ribs, white membrane removed
2 teaspoons salt
1 teaspoon ground black pepper
½ cup sriracha
⅓ cup honey
1 tablespoon lemon juice

1. Preheat the air fryer to 400°F.
2. Place ribs on a work surface and cut the rack into two pieces to fit in the air fryer basket.
3. Sprinkle ribs with salt and pepper and place in the air fryer basket meat side down. Cook 15 minutes.
4. In a small bowl, combine the sriracha, honey, and lemon juice to make a sauce.
5. Remove ribs from the air fryer basket and pour sauce over both sides. Return them to the air fryer basket meat side up and cook an additional 10 minutes until brown and the internal temperature reaches at least 190°F. Serve warm.

PER SERVING

CALORIES: 600 | **FAT:** 35g | **PROTEIN:** 42g | **SODIUM:** 2,180mg | **FIBER:** 1g | **CARBOHYDRATES:** 31g | **SUGAR:** 29g

Brown Sugar Mustard Pork Loin

Pork loin is lean and mild tasting, which means it goes well with a variety of flavors. This recipe is both tangy and sweet in a deliciously balanced way. The brown sugar creates crispy darkened bits that go perfectly with the mustard flavor that has soaked into the meat.

Pantry Staples: salt, ground black pepper
Hands-On Time: 5 minutes
Cook Time: 35 minutes

Serves 4

- 1 pound boneless pork loin
- 1 tablespoon olive oil
- ¼ cup Dijon mustard
- ¼ cup brown sugar
- 1 teaspoon salt
- ½ teaspoon ground black pepper

1. Preheat the air fryer to 400°F. Brush pork loin with oil.
2. In a small bowl, mix mustard, brown sugar, salt, and pepper. Brush mixture over both sides of pork loin and let sit 15 minutes.
3. Place in the air fryer basket and cook 20 minutes until internal temperature reaches 145°F. Let rest 10 minutes before slicing. Serve warm.

PER SERVING

CALORIES: 250 | **FAT:** 12g | **PROTEIN:** 21g | **SODIUM:** 1,270mg | **FIBER:** 0g | **CARBOHYDRATES:** 13g | **SUGAR:** 13g

Beef Short Ribs

Short ribs have a flavor similar to roast, which make them an excellent comfort food. Traditionally, they're braised to preserve their flavor and moisture, but in the air fryer you can get that delicious roasted flavor in just 30 minutes. The sauce locks in the moisture and gives you a tasty meal that your whole family will enjoy.

Pantry Staples: salt, ground black pepper
Hands-On Time: 5 minutes
Cook Time: 25 minutes

Serves 4

- 3 pounds beef short ribs
- 2 tablespoons olive oil
- 3 teaspoons salt
- 3 teaspoons ground black pepper
- ½ cup barbecue sauce

1. Preheat the air fryer to 375°F.
2. Place short ribs in a large bowl. Drizzle with oil and sprinkle both sides with salt and pepper.
3. Place in the air fryer basket and cook 20 minutes. Remove from basket and brush with barbecue sauce. Return to the air fryer basket and cook 5 additional minutes until sauce is dark brown and internal temperature reaches at least 160°F. Serve warm.

PER SERVING

CALORIES: 1,080 | **FAT:** 97g | **PROTEIN:** 36g | **SODIUM:** 1,630mg | **FIBER:** 0g | **CARBOHYDRATES:** 14g | **SUGAR:** 11g

Cheeseburgers

This classic dinner couldn't be easier with the air fryer. The burgers get browned on the top while remaining extra juicy in the middle. Feel free to customize these burgers to your liking by adding more seasonings as well as your favorite toppings, such as lettuce, tomatoes, or even bacon.

Pantry Staples: salt, ground black pepper
Hands-On Time: 5 minutes
Cook Time: 10 minutes

Serves 4

- **1 pound 70/30 ground beef**
- **½ teaspoon salt**
- **¼ teaspoon ground black pepper**
- **4 (1-ounce) slices American cheese**
- **4 hamburger buns**

1. Preheat the air fryer to 360°F.
2. Separate beef into four equal portions and form into patties.
3. Sprinkle both sides of patties with salt and pepper. Place in the air fryer basket and cook 10 minutes, turning halfway through cooking time, until internal temperature reaches at least 160°F.
4. For each burger, place a slice of cheese on a patty and place on a hamburger bun. Serve warm.

PER SERVING

CALORIES: 590 | **FAT:** 43g | **PROTEIN:** 25g | **SODIUM:** 990mg | **FIBER:** 0g | **CARBOHYDRATES:** 25g | **SUGAR:** 5g

RESTAURANT-STYLE BARBECUE BURGER

Try using a pretzel bun and adding sharp Cheddar cheese, bacon, barbecue sauce, and a fried onion ring on top for a deliciously flavorful meal.

Ground Beef

This might just become your new favorite way to brown your ground beef. You'll be surprised at how tender and easily broken up your ground beef comes out. You'll need to stir it just a few times during cooking, but the result is worth it. Use this method for any recipe in which you need to cook ground beef, such as tacos, empanadas, burritos, or casseroles.

Pantry Staples: salt, ground black pepper
Hands-On Time: 5 minutes
Cook Time: 9 minutes

Serves 4

1 pound 70/30 ground beef
¼ cup water
1 teaspoon salt
½ teaspoon ground black pepper
1 teaspoon garlic powder

1. Preheat the air fryer to 400°F.
2. In a medium bowl, mix beef with remaining ingredients. Place beef in a 6" round cake pan and press into an even layer.
3. Place in the air fryer basket and set the timer to 10 minutes. After 5 minutes, open the air fryer and stir ground beef with a spatula. Return to the air fryer.
4. After 2 more minutes, open the air fryer, remove the pan and drain any excess fat from the ground beef. Return to the air fryer for and cook 2 more minutes until beef is brown and no pink remains.

PER SERVING

CALORIES: 380 | **FAT:** 34g | **PROTEIN:** 16g | **SODIUM:** 660mg | **FIBER:** 0g | **CARBOHYDRATES:** 1g | **SUGAR:** 0g

Hot Dogs

There are so many ways to cook hot dogs, from boiling them on the stove to grilling them. Popping them in the air fryer is one of the easiest ways to achieve juicy hot dogs with that crisp outside. This meal is a lifesaver because it's easy and requires no preparation other than preheating the air fryer. Try adding toppings such as chopped onions, pickled jalapeños, or even banana peppers for a flavorful take on this easy classic.

Pantry Staples: none
Hands-On Time: 5 minutes
Cook Time: 7 minutes

Serves 8

8 (3.5-ounce) beef hot dogs
8 hot dog buns

1 Preheat the air fryer to 400°F.

2 Place hot dogs in the air fryer basket and cook 7 minutes. Place each hot dog in a bun. Serve warm.

PER SERVING

CALORIES: 470 | **FAT:** 31g | **PROTEIN:** 16g | **SODIUM:** 1,340mg | **FIBER:** 0g | **CARBOHYDRATES:** 31g | **SUGAR:** 7g

Bacon Blue Cheese Burger

This burger with a tang is perfect for switching things up without much effort. Each bite is loaded with the deliciousness of blue cheese and bacon.

Pantry Staples: salt, ground black pepper
Hands-On Time: 5 minutes
Cook Time: 15 minutes

Serves 4

1 pound ground sirloin
½ cup crumbled blue cheese
8 slices bacon, cooked and crumbled
1 teaspoon Worcestershire sauce
1 teaspoon salt
½ teaspoon ground black pepper
4 pretzel buns

1 Preheat the air fryer to 370°F.

2 In a large bowl, mix sirloin, cheese, bacon, and Worcestershire until well combined.

3 Form into four patties and sprinkle each side with salt and pepper. Spritz with cooking spray and place in the air fryer basket.

4 Cook 15 minutes, turning halfway through cooking time, until internal temperature reaches at least 160°F for well-done. Place on pretzel buns to serve.

PER SERVING

CALORIES: 680 | **FAT:** 43g | **PROTEIN:** 40g | **SODIUM:** 1,990mg | **FIBER:** 0g | **CARBOHYDRATES:** 28g | **SUGAR:** 2g

Jumbo Italian Meatballs

These meatballs are delicious on their own and also make the perfect addition to any pasta meal. Try enjoying them as a meatball grinder by sandwiching them between slices of your favorite toasted bread and topping with a few tablespoons of marinara and a slice of provolone cheese.

Pantry Staples: salt, ground black pepper
Hands-On Time: 10 minutes
Cook Time: 15 minutes

Serves 6

1 pound 80/20 ground beef
⅓ cup Italian bread crumbs
1 large egg
2 teaspoons Italian seasoning
¼ cup grated Parmesan cheese
1 teaspoon salt
½ teaspoon ground black pepper

1. Preheat the air fryer to 400°F.
2. In a large bowl, mix all the ingredients. Roll mixture into balls, about 3" each, making twelve total.
3. Place meatballs in the air fryer basket and cook 15 minutes, shaking the basket twice during cooking, until meatballs are brown on the outside and internal temperature reaches at least 160°F. Serve warm.

PER SERVING (SERVING SIZE: 2 MEATBALLS)

CALORIES: 240 | **FAT:** 1g | **PROTEIN:** 16g | **SODIUM:** 600mg | **FIBER:** 0g | **CARBOHYDRATES:** 5g | **SUGAR:** 0g

Meatloaf

Meatloaf is an easy, classic comfort food. The juicy beef is covered in a dark caramelized glaze that makes every bite delicious. This dish goes great with Fried Mashed Potato Balls in Chapter 4.

Pantry Staples: salt
Hands-On Time: 10 minutes
Cook Time: 40 minutes

Serves 4

1 pound 80/20 lean ground beef
1 large egg
3 tablespoons Italian bread crumbs
1 teaspoon salt
2 tablespoons ketchup
2 tablespoons brown sugar

1. Preheat the air fryer to 350°F.
2. In a large bowl, combine beef, egg, bread crumbs, and salt.
3. In a small bowl, mix ketchup and brown sugar.
4. Form meat mixture into a 6" × 3" loaf and brush with ketchup mixture.
5. Place in the air fryer basket and cook 40 minutes until internal temperature reaches at least 160°F. Serve warm.

PER SERVING

CALORIES: 360 | **FAT:** 24g | **PROTEIN:** 22g | **SODIUM:** 830mg | **FIBER:** 0g | **CARBOHYDRATES:** 13g | **SUGAR:** 10g

Stuffed Peppers

The best stuffed peppers are tender without being mushy, and that's incredibly easy to achieve in the air fryer. By using canned diced tomatoes and chilies, you'll save time without sacrificing taste. These flavorful peppers are filled with juicy sausage and gooey melted cheese in every bite.

Pantry Staples: salt
Hands-On Time: 10 minutes
Cook Time: 15 minutes

Serves 4

- ½ pound cooked Italian sausage, drained
- 1 (10-ounce) can diced tomatoes and green chilies, drained
- 2 teaspoons Italian seasoning
- 1 teaspoon salt
- 4 large green bell peppers, trimmed and seeded
- 1 cup shredded Italian-blend cheese

1. Preheat the air fryer to 320°F.
2. In a large bowl, mix sausage, tomatoes and chilies, Italian seasoning, and salt.
3. Spoon one-fourth of meat mixture into each pepper. Sprinkle ¼ cup cheese on top of each pepper. Spritz peppers with cooking spray and place in the air fryer basket.
4. Cook 15 minutes until peppers are tender and cheese is melted and bubbling. Serve warm.

PER SERVING

CALORIES: 280 | **FAT:** 19g | **PROTEIN:** 16g | **SODIUM:** 1,460mg | **FIBER:** 3g | **CARBOHYDRATES:** 12g | **SUGAR:** 6g

ADD RICE

Try adding a cup of cooked long grain white rice to the mixture before stuffing the peppers for an even more filling meal. For an extra helping of vegetables, you can use steamed riced cauliflower.

Rib Eye Steak

The air fryer is great for easily cooking juicy and delicious steaks, and a digital meat thermometer will be your best aid in achieving your preferred doneness. Look for a thermometer with a probe on a wire so that you can place it in the air fryer and close the lid to monitor the temperature in real time as the meat cooks.

Pantry Staples: salt, ground black pepper
Hands-On Time: 5 minutes
Cook Time: 15 minutes

Serves 4

4 (6-ounce) rib eye steaks
1 teaspoon salt
½ teaspoon ground black pepper
2 tablespoons salted butter

1. Preheat the air fryer to 400°F.
2. Sprinkle steaks with salt and pepper and place in the air fryer basket.
3. Cook 15 minutes, turning halfway through cooking time, until edges are firm, and the internal temperature reaches at least 160°F for well-done.
4. Top each steak with ½ tablespoon butter immediately after removing from the air fryer. Let rest 5 minutes before cutting. Serve warm.

PER SERVING

CALORIES: 280 | **FAT:** 14g | **PROTEIN:** 39g | **SODIUM:** 740mg | **FIBER:** 0g | **CARBOHYDRATES:** 0g | **SUGAR:** 0g

Steak Bites and Spicy Dipping Sauce

This protein-centered dish is perfect for a filling dinner or even a snack to keep you going all day. These bites cook up in just minutes and stay tender and juicy on the inside while getting deliciously dark brown edges. The creamy sauce has just a hint of heat that really takes these bites to the next level.

Pantry Staples: salt, ground black pepper
Hands-On Time: 5 minutes
Cook Time: 8 minutes

Serves 4

- **2 pounds sirloin steak, cut into 2" cubes**
- **2 teaspoons salt**
- **1 teaspoon ground black pepper**
- **1 teaspoon garlic powder**
- **½ cup mayonnaise**
- **2 tablespoons sriracha**

1. Preheat the air fryer to 400°F.
2. Sprinkle steak with salt, pepper, and garlic powder.
3. Place steak in the air fryer basket and cook 8 minutes, shaking the basket twice during cooking, until internal temperature reaches at least 160°F.
4. In a small bowl, combine mayonnaise and sriracha. Serve with steak bites for dipping.

PER SERVING

CALORIES: 690 | **FAT:** 53g | **PROTEIN:** 46g | **SODIUM:** 1,660mg | **FIBER:** 0g | **CARBOHYDRATES:** 3g | **SUGAR:** 2g

Steak Kebabs

When you don't have the time to fire up the grill or it's just too cold outside, the air fryer is a great way to enjoy kebabs all year long. Cooking the meat and vegetables on skewers helps marry the flavors, making for a delicious meal. The steak pieces cook quickly without drying out, and the vegetables get beautiful caramelized edges just like the grilled variety.

Pantry Staples: salt, ground black pepper
Hands-On Time: 15 minutes
Cook Time: 10 minutes per batch

Serves 4

- **1½ pounds sirloin steak, cut into 1" cubes**
- **1 medium yellow onion, peeled and cut into 1" pieces**
- **1 medium green bell pepper, seeded and cut into 1" pieces**
- **1 medium red bell pepper, seeded and cut into 1" pieces**
- **1 teaspoon salt**
- **½ teaspoon ground black pepper**
- **2 tablespoons olive oil**

1. Soak twelve 6" skewers in water 10 minutes to prevent burning. Preheat the air fryer to 400°F.
2. To assemble kebabs, place one piece of steak on skewer, then a piece of onion, green bell pepper, and red bell pepper. Repeat three times per skewer.
3. Sprinkle assembled kebabs with salt and black pepper, then drizzle with oil.
4. Place kebabs in the air fryer basket in a single layer, working in batches as necessary. Cook 10 minutes, turning halfway through cooking time, until vegetables are tender, meat is brown, and internal temperature reaches at least 160°F. Serve warm.

PER SERVING (SERVING SIZE: 3 KEBABS)

CALORIES: 450 | **FAT:** 31g | **PROTEIN:** 35g | **SODIUM:** 670mg | **FIBER:** 2g | **CARBOHYDRATES:** 6g | **SUGAR:** 3g

Calzones

The secret to amazing calzones is all in the filling. The mix of cheeses makes every bite soft and delicious. An egg wash gives this dish a deep golden crust that stays light and pillowy on the side and is perfect for dipping in sauce.

Pantry Staples: none
Hands-On Time: 10 minutes
Cook Time: 15 minutes

Serves 4

1 (13.8-ounce) tube refrigerated pizza dough
28 slices pepperoni
½ cup full-fat ricotta cheese
1 cup shredded mozzarella cheese
1 large egg, whisked

1. Preheat the air fryer to 350°F. Cut parchment paper to fit the air fryer basket.
2. Place dough on a work surface and unroll. Cut into four sections.
3. For each calzone, place 7 slices pepperoni on the bottom half of a dough section. Top pepperoni with 2 tablespoons ricotta and ¼ cup mozzarella.
4. Fold top half of dough over to cover the fillings and press the edges together. Gently roll the edges closed or press them with a fork to seal.
5. Brush calzones with egg. Place on parchment in the air fryer basket and cook 15 minutes, turning after about 10 minutes, until firm and golden brown. Serve warm.

PER SERVING

CALORIES: 460 | **FAT:** 20g | **PROTEIN:** 23g | **SODIUM:** 1,030mg | **FIBER:** 0g | **CARBOHYDRATES:** 49g | **SUGAR:** 6g

MAKE IT YOUR OWN

Fill these calzones with all your favorite pizza toppings. Ground beef, ham, onions, and peppers are delicious additions. For a restaurant-style calzone, brush with melted butter after cooking and sprinkle with Parmesan and Italian seasoning.

Spinach and Mushroom Steak Rolls

Savory vegetables elevate this steak meal to a whole new level. Don't worry about the steak becoming dry; the natural fats keep it juicy and delicious, similar to cooking in the oven. The edges darken and fill with melted cheese, making every bite delicious.

Pantry Staples: salt, ground black pepper

Hands-On Time: 15 minutes

Cook Time: 19 minutes

Serves 4

- **½ medium yellow onion, peeled and chopped**
- **½ cup chopped baby bella mushrooms**
- **1 cup chopped fresh spinach**
- **1 pound flank steak**
- **8 (1-ounce) slices provolone cheese**
- **1 teaspoon salt**
- **½ teaspoon ground black pepper**

1. In a medium skillet over medium heat, sauté onion 2 minutes until fragrant and beginning to soften. Add mushrooms and spinach and continue cooking 5 more minutes until spinach is wilted and mushrooms are soft.
2. Preheat the air fryer to 400°F.
3. Carefully butterfly steak, leaving the two halves connected. Place slices of cheese on top of steak, then top with cooked vegetables.
4. Place steak so that the grain runs horizontally. Tightly roll up steak and secure it closed with eight evenly placed toothpicks or eight sections of butcher's twine.
5. Slice steak into four rolls. Spritz with cooking spray, then sprinkle with salt and pepper. Place in the air fryer basket and cook 12 minutes until steak is brown on the edges and internal temperature reaches at least 160°F for well-done. Serve.

PER SERVING

CALORIES: 360 | **FAT:** 21g | **PROTEIN:** 37g | **SODIUM:** 950mg | **FIBER:** 1g | **CARBOHYDRATES:** 2g | **SUGAR:** 37g

Fajita Flank Steak Rolls

This spin on steak fajitas might just become your new favorite. This meal has all the great flavors of fajitas cooked in less than 15 minutes. The vegetables caramelize at the edges for a tasty, sweet flavor.

Pantry Staples: salt, ground black pepper
Hands-On Time: 10 minutes
Cook Time: 12 minutes

Serves 4

- 1 pound flank steak
- 4 (1-ounce) slices pepper jack cheese
- 1 medium green bell pepper, seeded and chopped
- ½ medium red bell pepper, seeded and chopped
- ¼ cup finely chopped yellow onion
- 1 teaspoon salt
- ½ teaspoon ground black pepper

1. Preheat the air fryer to 400°F.
2. Carefully butterfly steak, leaving the two halves connected. Place slices of cheese on top of steak. Scatter bell peppers and onion over cheese in an even layer.
3. Place steak so that the grain runs horizontally. Tightly roll up steak and secure it with eight evenly spaced toothpicks or eight sections of butcher's twine.
4. Slice steak into four even rolls. Spritz with cooking spray, then sprinkle with salt and black pepper. Place in the air fryer basket and cook 12 minutes until steak is brown on the edges and internal temperature reaches at least 160°F for well-done. Serve.

PER SERVING

CALORIES: 280 | **FAT:** 15g | **PROTEIN:** 30g | **SODIUM:** 790mg | **FIBER:** 1g | **CARBOHYDRATES:** 3g | **SUGAR:** 30g

Orange and Brown Sugar–Glazed Ham

This glaze is perfect for finishing off your holiday ham. Just mix the ingredients, pop it in your air fryer, and you're ready to serve! The sugars caramelize and form a delicious crust while the juice gets into the meat and adds a wonderfully light flavor.

Pantry Staples: salt, ground black pepper
Hands-On Time: 5 minutes
Cook Time: 15 minutes

Serves 8

- ½ cup brown sugar
- ¼ cup orange juice
- 2 tablespoons yellow mustard
- 1 (4-pound) fully cooked boneless ham
- 1 teaspoon salt
- ½ teaspoon ground black pepper

1. Preheat the air fryer to 375°F.
2. In a medium bowl, whisk together brown sugar, orange juice, and mustard until combined. Brush over ham until well coated. Sprinkle with salt and pepper.
3. Place in the air fryer basket and cook 15 minutes until heated through and edges are caramelized. Serve warm.

PER SERVING

CALORIES: 390 | **FAT:** 17g | **PROTEIN:** 43g | **SODIUM:** 2,960mg | **FIBER:** 0g | **CARBOHYDRATES:** 13g | **SUGAR:** 13g

Empanadas

These handhelds are both delicious and perfect for dipping. The flaky crust gives you a delicious buttery crunch, while the inside is packed with flavor and gooey melted cheese. Try dipping these in sour cream, salsa, or guacamole.

Pantry Staples: none
Hands-On Time: 10 minutes
Cook Time: 28 minutes

Serves 4

1 pound 80/20 ground beef
¼ cup taco seasoning
⅓ cup salsa
2 (9") refrigerated piecrusts
1 cup shredded Colby-jack cheese

1. In a medium skillet over medium heat, brown beef about 10 minutes until cooked through. Drain fat, then add taco seasoning and salsa to the pan. Bring to a boil, then cook 30 seconds. Reduce heat and simmer 5 minutes. Remove from heat.
2. Preheat the air fryer to 370°F.
3. Cut three 5" circles from each piecrust, forming six total. Reroll scraps out to ½" thickness. Cut out two more 5" circles to make eight circles total.
4. For each empanada, place ¼ cup meat mixture onto the lower half of a pastry circle and top with 2 tablespoons cheese. Dab a little water along the edge of pastry and fold circle in half to fully cover meat and cheese, pressing the edges together. Use a fork to gently seal the edges. Repeat with remaining pastry, meat, and cheese.
5. Spritz empanadas with cooking spray. Place in the air fryer basket and cook 12 minutes, turning halfway through cooking time, until crust is golden. Serve warm.

PER SERVING

CALORIES: 800 | **FAT:** 53g | **PROTEIN:** 31g | **SODIUM:** 980mg | **FIBER:** 0g | **CARBOHYDRATES:** 47g | **SUGAR:** 5g

CUSTOMIZE IT

Give this meal your own spin by switching out the filling. You can add any cooked chopped meat of your choice and your favorite vegetables. Bacon, Cheddar, and ranch or even eggs, sausage, and cheese would combine for a tasty breakfast.

Buttery Pork Chops

These simple pork chops are an excellent weeknight staple. They're brown and crispy while staying juicy on the inside, and the butter and a light seasoning provide a ton of flavor. These pork chops make a delicious meal that goes with just about any side dish.

Pantry Staples: salt, ground black pepper
Hands-On Time: 5 minutes
Cook Time: 12 minutes

Serves 4

- 4 (4-ounce) boneless pork chops
- 1 teaspoon salt
- ½ teaspoon ground black pepper
- 4 tablespoons salted butter, sliced into 8 (½-tablespoon) pats, divided

1. Preheat the air fryer to 400°F.
2. Sprinkle pork chops with salt and pepper. Top each pork chop with a ½-tablespoon butter pat.
3. Place chops in the air fryer basket and cook 12 minutes, turning halfway through cooking time, until tops and edges are golden brown and internal temperature reaches at least 145°F.
4. Use remaining butter pats to top each pork chop while hot, then let cool 5 minutes before serving warm.

PER SERVING

CALORIES: 300 | **FAT:** 26g | **PROTEIN:** 24g | **SODIUM:** 770mg | **FIBER:** 0g | **CARBOHYDRATES:** 0g | **SUGAR:** 0g

Crouton-Breaded Pork Chops

Croutons are full of flavor and make a great breading for pork chops. If you're a fan of stuffing, you'll love this breadlike crust. This is a great recipe for using up stale bread. See the recipe in Chapter 3 to make a quick batch of Croutons in your air fryer.

Pantry Staples: salt, ground black pepper
Hands-On Time: 10 minutes
Cook Time: 14 minutes

Serves 4

- **4 (4-ounce) boneless pork chops**
- **1 teaspoon salt**
- **½ teaspoon ground black pepper**
- **2 cups croutons**
- **½ teaspoon dried thyme**
- **¼ teaspoon dried sage**
- **1 large egg, whisked**

1. Preheat the air fryer to 400°F.
2. Sprinkle pork chops with salt and pepper on both sides.
3. In a food processor, add croutons, thyme, and sage. Pulse five times until croutons are mostly broken down with a few medium-sized pieces remaining. Transfer to a medium bowl.
4. In a separate medium bowl, place egg. Dip each pork chop into egg, then press into crouton mixture to coat both sides. Spritz with cooking spray.
5. Place pork in the air fryer basket and cook 14 minutes, turning halfway through cooking time, until chops are golden brown and internal temperature reaches at least 145°F. Serve warm.

PER SERVING

CALORIES: 310 | **FAT:** 17g | **PROTEIN:** 27g | **SODIUM:** 800mg | **FIBER:** 0g | **CARBOHYDRATES:** 12g | **SUGAR:** 0g

Cheddar Bacon Ranch Pinwheels

These fluffy pinwheels are a fun and filling meal. They're bursting with ranch flavor and have crispy bacon in every bite.

Pantry Staples: none
Hands-On Time: 10 minutes
Cook Time: 12 minutes per batch

Serves 5

4 ounces full-fat cream cheese, softened
1 tablespoon dry ranch seasoning
½ cup shredded Cheddar cheese
1 (8-ounce) sheet frozen puff pastry dough, thawed
6 slices bacon, cooked and crumbled

1. Preheat the air fryer to 320°F. Cut parchment paper to fit the air fryer basket.
2. In a medium bowl, mix cream cheese, ranch seasoning, and Cheddar. Unfold puff pastry and gently spread cheese mixture over pastry.
3. Sprinkle crumbled bacon on top. Starting from a long side, roll dough into a log, pressing in the edges to seal.
4. Cut log into ten pieces, then place on parchment in the air fryer basket, working in batches as necessary.
5. Cook 12 minutes, turning each piece after 7 minutes. Let cool 5 minutes before serving.

PER SERVING (SERVING SIZE: 2 PINWHEELS)

CALORIES: 350 | **FAT:** 26g | **PROTEIN:** 10g | **SODIUM:** 700mg | **FIBER:** 0g | **CARBOHYDRATES:** 17g | **SUGAR:** 2g

7

Fish and Seafood Main Dishes

Seafood is known for being notoriously difficult to cook. Of course it's delicious to eat, but if you're not careful, cooking these delicate dishes can quickly go south. Enter your air fryer. Even if you're a total beginner at cooking fish and seafood, your air fryer will take care of the guesswork and bring you the perfectly crisp, fresh, and flavorful meals you crave. From Bacon-Wrapped Cajun Scallops to Honey-Glazed Salmon, this chapter is a sea of amazing recipes you won't be able to get enough of!

Fish Taco Bowl

This meal is perfect for busy weeknights. It's quick and easy to make with lots of flavor. The crunchy and creamy slaw is the perfect companion for the spicy fish. If you enjoy extra spice, try adding pickled jalapeño pepper slices on top.

Pantry Staples: salt, ground black pepper
Hands-On Time: 10 minutes
Cook Time: 12 minutes

Serves 4

2 cups finely shredded cabbage
½ cup mayonnaise
Juice of 1 medium lime, divided
4 (6-ounce) boneless, skinless tilapia fillets
2 teaspoons chili powder
1 teaspoon salt
½ teaspoon ground black pepper

1. In a large bowl, mix cabbage, mayonnaise, and half of lime juice to make a slaw. Cover and refrigerate while the fish cooks.
2. Preheat the air fryer to 400°F.
3. Sprinkle tilapia with chili powder, salt, and pepper. Spritz each side with cooking spray.
4. Place fillets in the air fryer basket and cook 12 minutes, turning halfway through cooking time, until fish is opaque, flakes easily, and reaches an internal temperature of 145°F.
5. Allow fish to cool 5 minutes before chopping into bite-sized pieces. To serve, place ½ cup slaw into each bowl and top with one-fourth of fish. Squeeze remaining lime juice over fish. Serve warm.

PER SERVING

CALORIES: 370 | **FAT:** 24g | **PROTEIN:** 35g | **SODIUM:** 910mg | **FIBER:** 2g | **CARBOHYDRATES:** 5g | **SUGAR:** 2g

Crab Cakes

This recipe puts the crab center stage and lets the flavor shine. These cakes are crispy at the edges while staying soft and tender in the middle. While they may not be as firm as traditional crab cakes, they make up for it in flavor.

Pantry Staples: salt, ground black pepper
Hands-On Time: 10 minutes
Cook Time: 12 minutes

Serves 4

2 (6-ounce) cans lump crabmeat, drained
½ cup plain bread crumbs
½ cup mayonnaise
1½ teaspoons Old Bay Seasoning
Zest and juice of ½ medium lemon
½ teaspoon salt
½ teaspoon ground black pepper

1. Preheat the air fryer to 375°F.
2. In a large bowl, mix all ingredients.
3. Scoop ¼ cup mixture and form into a 4" patty. Repeat to make eight crab cakes. Spritz cakes with cooking spray.
4. Place in the air fryer basket and cook 12 minutes, turning halfway through cooking time, until edges are brown and center is firm. Serve warm.

PER SERVING (SERVING SIZE: 2 CAKES)

CALORIES: 300 | **FAT:** 23g | **PROTEIN:** 18g | **SODIUM:** 1,630mg | **FIBER:** 0g | **CARBOHYDRATES:** 10g | **SUGAR:** 1g

DIPPING SAUCE

If you like a creamy, spicy sauce, try making a sriracha mayonnaise to drizzle over the cakes. Whisk ½ cup mayonnaise with 2 teaspoons sriracha and ½ teaspoon soy sauce until smooth.

Bacon-Wrapped Cajun Scallops

Paired with a spicy Cajun seasoning, these scallops really sing. Bacon is an excellent way to add more flavor to your seafood, and partially cooking it before the main ingredient is an easy way to avoid overcooking the seafood.

Pantry Staples: none
Hands-On Time: 5 minutes
Cook Time: 13 minutes

Serves 4

8 slices bacon
8 (1-ounce) sea scallops, rinsed and patted dry
1 teaspoon Cajun seasoning
4 tablespoons salted butter, melted

1. Preheat the air fryer to 375°F.
2. Place bacon in the air fryer basket and cook 3 minutes. Remove bacon and wrap each scallop in one slice bacon before securing with a toothpick.
3. Sprinkle Cajun seasoning evenly over scallops. Spritz scallops lightly with cooking spray and place in the air fryer basket in a single layer. Cook 10 minutes, turning halfway through cooking time, until scallops are opaque and firm and internal temperature reaches at least 130°F. Drizzle with butter. Serve warm.

PER SERVING

CALORIES: 400 | **FAT:** 32g | **PROTEIN:** 23g | **SODIUM:** 1,370mg | **FIBER:** 0g | **CARBOHYDRATES:** 4g | **SUGAR:** 2g

Garlic-Lemon Scallops

There's no need to be intimidated when preparing scallops. This recipe is easy, delicious, and is much cheaper than ordering them in a restaurant. Though they are a delicate seafood, scallops don't require much attention in the air fryer. They come out juicy and tender with brown edges similar to when they're pan seared.

Pantry Staples: salt, ground black pepper
Hands-On Time: 5 minutes
Cook Time: 12 minutes

Serves 4

¼ teaspoon salt
¼ teaspoon ground black pepper
8 (1-ounce) sea scallops, rinsed and patted dry
4 tablespoons salted butter, melted
4 teaspoons finely minced garlic
Zest and juice of ½ small lemon

WHERE TO FIND SCALLOPS

You can usually find fresh scallops in your local grocery store's fresh seafood department. You may be able to find frozen scallops in the freezer section as well. To thaw, simply place the scallops in a bowl of cool water 5 minutes until the scallops are soft.

1. Preheat the air fryer to 375°F.
2. Sprinkle salt and pepper evenly over scallops. Spritz scallops lightly with cooking spray. Place in the air fryer basket in a single layer and cook 12 minutes, turning halfway through cooking time, until scallops are opaque and firm and internal temperature reaches at least 130°F.
3. While scallops are cooking, in a small bowl, mix butter, garlic, lemon zest, and juice. Set aside.
4. When scallops are done, drizzle with garlic-lemon butter. Serve warm.

PER SERVING

CALORIES: 160 | **FAT:** 12g | **PROTEIN:** 7g | **SODIUM:** 460mg | **FIBER:** 0g | **CARBOHYDRATES:** 2g | **SUGAR:** 0g

Cod Nuggets

If you were a fan of fish sticks as a kid, you'll love this recipe. Cod is a mild fish, which makes it the perfect flavor for these nuggets. They're crispy and golden on the outside and flaky on the inside. Try adding ½ teaspoon of your favorite seasoning to the bread crumbs for an extra burst of flavor.

Pantry Staples: salt, ground black pepper
Hands-On Time: 10 minutes
Cook Time: 12 minutes

Serves 4

2 (6-ounce) boneless, skinless cod fillets
1½ teaspoons salt, divided
¾ teaspoon ground black pepper, divided
2 large eggs
1 cup plain bread crumbs

1. Preheat the air fryer to 350°F.
2. Cut cod fillets into sixteen even-sized pieces. In a large bowl, add cod nuggets and sprinkle with 1 teaspoon salt and ½ teaspoon pepper.
3. In a small bowl, whisk eggs. In another small bowl, mix bread crumbs with remaining ½ teaspoon salt and ¼ teaspoon pepper.
4. One by one, dip nuggets in the eggs, shaking off excess before rolling in the bread crumb mixture. Repeat to make sixteen nuggets.
5. Place nuggets in the air fryer basket and spritz with cooking spray. Cook 12 minutes, turning halfway through cooking time. Nuggets will be done when golden brown and have an internal temperature of at least 145°F. Serve warm.

PER SERVING (SERVING SIZE: 4 NUGGETS)

CALORIES: 220 | **FAT:** 4g | **PROTEIN:** 22g | **SODIUM:** 1,110mg | **FIBER:** 0g | **CARBOHYDRATES:** 20g | **SUGAR:** 2g

Potato-Crusted Cod

This golden-crusted fish is mild but full of flavor. The crust makes a crunchy complement to the fresh-tasting cod. Pair this dish with any roasted or steamed vegetable for the perfect quick meal.

Pantry Staples: salt
Hands-On Time: 10 minutes
Cook Time: 15 minutes

Serves 4

4 (4-ounce) boneless, skinless cod fillets
2 tablespoons olive oil
½ teaspoon salt, divided
1 teaspoon dried dill
2 cups mashed potato flakes

1. Preheat the air fryer to 350°F.
2. Place cod fillets on a work surface and brush with oil. Sprinkle with ¼ teaspoon salt and dill.
3. In a large bowl, combine mashed potato flakes with remaining salt.
4. Roll each fillet in the potato mixture and spritz with cooking spray.
5. Place in the air fryer basket and cook 15 minutes, turning halfway through cooking time. Cod will be golden brown and have an internal temperature of at least 145°F when done. Serve warm.

PER SERVING

CALORIES: 240 | **FAT:** 8g | **PROTEIN:** 22g | **SODIUM:** 370mg | **FIBER:** 0g | **CARBOHYDRATES:** 21g | **SUGAR:** 2g

Chili-Lime Shrimp

Whether you're a longtime fan of shrimp or interested in learning to cook it for the first time, this recipe is perfect. If you don't like sriracha, feel free to substitute 1 teaspoon chili powder.

Pantry Staples: salt, ground black pepper
Hands-On Time: 5 minutes
Cook Time: 10 minutes

Serves 4

1 pound medium shrimp, peeled and deveined
½ cup lime juice
2 tablespoons olive oil
2 tablespoons sriracha
1 teaspoon salt
¼ teaspoon ground black pepper

1. Preheat the air fryer to 375°F.
2. In an 6" round cake pan, combine all ingredients.
3. Place pan in the air fryer and cook 10 minutes, stirring halfway through cooking time, until the inside of shrimp are pearly white and opaque and internal temperature reaches at least 145°F. Serve warm.

PER SERVING

CALORIES: 160 | **FAT:** 8g | **PROTEIN:** 16g | **SODIUM:** 1,430mg | **FIBER:** 0g | **CARBOHYDRATES:** 6g | **SUGAR:** 2g

Salmon Patties

This recipe is a delicious way to get your seafood fix. It takes less than 5 minutes to mix up delicious patties that make the perfect weeknight meal. The crispy golden edges give them a much-needed texture that complements the soft, moist center.

Pantry Staples: none
Hands-On Time: 5 minutes
Cook Time: 12 minutes

Serves 4

1 (10-ounce) pouch cooked salmon
6 tablespoons panko bread crumbs
½ cup mayonnaise
2 teaspoons Old Bay Seasoning

1. Preheat the air fryer to 350°F.
2. In a large bowl, combine all ingredients.
3. Divide mixture into four equal portions. Using your hands, form into patties and spritz with cooking spray.
4. Place in the air fryer basket and cook 12 minutes, turning halfway through cooking time, until brown and firm. Serve warm.

PER SERVING

CALORIES: 380 | **FAT:** 29g | **PROTEIN:** 21g | **SODIUM:** 430mg | **FIBER:** 0g | **CARBOHYDRATES:** 6g | **SUGAR:** 0g

Lemon Butter–Dill Salmon

This classic flavor combination is always a winner. Nothing goes with seafood like lemon and butter. This fresh combination is quick to pull together and goes with a variety of side dishes, from broccoli to roasted potatoes.

Pantry Staples: salt, ground black pepper
Hands-On Time: 5 minutes
Cook Time: 10 minutes

Serves 4

- 4 (6-ounce) skin-on salmon fillets
- ¾ teaspoon salt
- ½ teaspoon ground black pepper
- 1 medium lemon, halved
- 2 tablespoons salted butter, melted
- 1 teaspoon dried dill

1. Preheat the air fryer to 375°F.
2. Sprinkle salmon with salt and pepper.
3. Juice half the lemon and slice the other half into ¼"-thick pieces. In a small bowl, combine juice with butter. Brush mixture over salmon.
4. Sprinkle dill evenly over salmon. Place lemon slices on top of salmon.
5. Place salmon in the air fryer basket and cook 10 minutes until salmon flakes easily and internal temperature reaches at least 145°F. Remove lemon slices before serving.

PER SERVING

CALORIES: 280 | **FAT:** 14g | **PROTEIN:** 38g | **SODIUM:** 610mg | **FIBER:** 1g | **CARBOHYDRATES:** 2g | **SUGAR:** 1g

Honey-Glazed Salmon

Cooking seafood doesn't have to be complicated—this recipe marinates and cooks in about 30 minutes. If you're a fan of sweet and spicy, this will be your new go-to salmon.

Pantry Staples: none
Hands-On Time: 5 minutes
Cook Time: 30 minutes

Serves 4

2 tablespoons soy sauce
1 teaspoon sriracha
½ teaspoon minced garlic
4 (6-ounce) skin-on salmon fillets
2 teaspoons honey

1. In a large bowl, whisk together soy sauce, sriracha, and garlic. Place salmon in bowl. Cover and let marinate in refrigerator at least 20 minutes.
2. Preheat the air fryer to 375°F.
3. Place salmon in the air fryer basket and cook 8 minutes. Open air fryer and brush honey on salmon. Continue cooking 2 more minutes until salmon flakes easily and internal temperature reaches at least 145°F. Serve warm.

PER SERVING

CALORIES: 240 | **FAT:** 8g | **PROTEIN:** 35g | **SODIUM:** 740mg | **FIBER:** 0g | **CARBOHYDRATES:** 4g | **SUGAR:** 4g

REMOVING THE SKIN

Many people prefer skin-on salmon because it helps keep the fish from overcooking in the air fryer. This is totally fine, but not completely necessary. If you prefer a skinless variety, be sure to spray the air fryer basket with cooking spray prior to cooking to make sure the salmon fillets don't stick to the basket.

Lobster Tails

Lobster tails may seem like something to avoid cooking yourself, especially because they tend to be on the pricey side, but the good news is your air fryer makes preparing firm and fresh lobster tails, bursting with sweet and succulent flavor, easier than ever.

Pantry Staples: salt, ground black pepper
Hands-On Time: 5 minutes
Cook Time: 10 minutes

Serves 4

4 (6-ounce) lobster tails
2 tablespoons salted butter, melted
1 tablespoon finely minced garlic
¼ teaspoon salt
¼ teaspoon ground black pepper
2 tablespoons lemon juice

1. Preheat the air fryer to 400°F.
2. Carefully cut open lobster tails with kitchen scissors and pull back the shell a little to expose the meat. Drizzle butter over each tail, then sprinkle with garlic, salt, and pepper.
3. Place tails in the air fryer basket and cook 10 minutes until lobster is firm and opaque and internal temperature reaches at least 145°F.
4. Drizzle lemon juice over lobster meat. Serve warm.

PER SERVING

CALORIES: 200 | **FAT:** 7g | **PROTEIN:** 28g | **SODIUM:** 910mg | **FIBER:** 0g | **CARBOHYDRATES:** 1g | **SUGAR:** 0g

PREPARING LOBSTER TAILS AT HOME

If you haven't cut open a lobster tail before, it might be a little tricky, but it gets easier with practice. Don't be afraid to crack the shell apart to expose the meat, but be mindful of small, sharp pieces of shell that could break off.

Ahi Tuna Steaks

Fresh tuna steaks have a unique, delicate flavor that's best with light seasonings to really let it shine. The crust in this recipe gives the tuna a nice crunch, which really complements the smooth tuna texture. Everything bagel seasoning contains poppy seeds, sesame seeds, and dried onion flakes for an easy flavor add-on. If you don't like this seasoning, feel free to substitute sesame seeds.

Pantry Staples: none
Hands-On Time: 5 minutes
Cook Time: 14 minutes

Serves 2

2 (6-ounce) ahi tuna steaks
2 tablespoons olive oil
3 tablespoons everything bagel seasoning

INTERNAL TEMPERATURE
This recipe uses food safety guidelines to determine the internal temperature for doneness. Some prefer to enjoy fresh tuna steak rare or medium, with an internal temperature between 120°F and 130°F. If you're considering a different level of doneness, make sure you're using sushi-grade tuna.

1. Preheat the air fryer to 400°F.
2. Drizzle both sides of steaks with oil. Place seasoning on a medium plate and press each side of tuna steaks into seasoning to form a thick layer.
3. Place steaks in the air fryer basket and cook 14 minutes, turning halfway through cooking time, until internal temperature reaches at least 145°F for well-done. Serve warm.

PER SERVING

CALORIES: 360 | **FAT:** 22g | **PROTEIN:** 40g | **SODIUM:** 65mg | **FIBER:** 0g | **CARBOHYDRATES:** 0g | **SUGAR:** 0g

Snow Crab Legs

Making crab legs at home doesn't have to be intimidating. They're incredibly easy to make in the air fryer and can be ready in about 20 minutes. You'll love the sweet, fresh-tasting crab bites dipped in savory butter sauce. Just be sure you have a snow crab cracker handy to open them.

Pantry Staples: none
Hands-On Time: 5 minutes
Cook Time: 15 minutes per batch

Serves 6

- 8 pounds fresh shell-on snow crab legs
- 2 tablespoons olive oil
- 2 teaspoons Old Bay Seasoning
- 4 tablespoons salted butter, melted
- 2 teaspoons lemon juice

1. Preheat the air fryer to 400°F.
2. Drizzle crab legs with oil and sprinkle with Old Bay. Place in the air fryer basket, working in batches as necessary. Cook 15 minutes, turning halfway through cooking time, until crab turns a bright red-orange.
3. In a small bowl, whisk together butter and lemon juice. Serve as a dipping sauce with warm crab legs.

PER SERVING

CALORIES: 830 | **FAT:** 18g | **PROTEIN:** 145g | **SODIUM:** 4,370mg | **FIBER:** 0g | **CARBOHYDRATES:** 0g | **SUGAR:** 0g

Coconut Shrimp

If you're a fan of crunchy and juicy shrimp, this recipe is for you. These shrimp are golden on the outside and make the perfect meal or appetizer. Feel free to add ½ teaspoon of your favorite seasoning for a flavor boost.

Pantry Staples: all-purpose flour, salt
Hands-On Time: 10 minutes
Cook Time: 10 minutes

Serves 4

1 cup all-purpose flour
1 teaspoon salt
2 large eggs
½ cup panko bread crumbs
1 cup shredded unsweetened coconut flakes
1 pound large shrimp, peeled and deveined

1. Preheat the air fryer to 375°F.
2. In a medium bowl, mix flour and salt. In a separate medium bowl, whisk eggs. In a third medium bowl, mix bread crumbs and coconut flakes.
3. Dredge shrimp first in flour mixture, shaking off excess, then in eggs, letting any additional egg drip off, and finally in bread crumb mixture. Spritz with cooking spray.
4. Place shrimp in the air fryer basket. Cook 10 minutes, turning and spritzing opposite side with cooking spray halfway through cooking, until insides are pearly white and opaque and internal temperature reaches at least 145°F. Serve warm.

PER SERVING

CALORIES: 360 | **FAT:** 14g | **PROTEIN:** 24g | **SODIUM:** 1,280mg | **FIBER:** 3g | **CARBOHYDRATES:** 37g | **SUGAR:** 1g

Lemon Pepper–Breaded Tilapia

The lemon pepper seasoning is the star of this dish and brightens up the mild fish with the perfect zest.

Pantry Staples: all-purpose flour
Hands-On Time: 10 minutes
Cook Time: 10 minutes

Serves 4

- **1 large egg**
- **⅓ cup all-purpose flour**
- **¼ cup grated Parmesan cheese**
- **½ tablespoon lemon pepper seasoning**
- **4 (6-ounce) boneless, skinless tilapia fillets**

1. Preheat the air fryer to 375°F.
2. In a medium bowl, whisk egg. On a large plate, mix flour, Parmesan, and lemon pepper seasoning.
3. Pat tilapia dry. Dip each fillet into egg, gently shaking off excess. Press into flour mixture, then spritz both sides with cooking spray.
4. Place in the air fryer basket and cook 10 minutes, turning halfway through cooking, until fillets are golden and crispy and internal temperature reaches at least 145°F. Serve warm.

PER SERVING

CALORIES: 240 | **FAT:** 5g | **PROTEIN:** 38g | **SODIUM:** 320mg | **FIBER:** 38g | **CARBOHYDRATES:** 9g | **SUGAR:** 0g

Cajun Lobster Tails

If you love plump, juicy lobster with a little spice, then you'll love this recipe. This meal is great for busy weeknights and goes well with sides like the Macaroni and Cheese in Chapter 4.

Pantry Staples: none
Hands-On Time: 5 minutes
Cook Time: 10 minutes

Serves 4

- **4 (6-ounce) lobster tails**
- **2 tablespoons salted butter, melted**
- **2 teaspoons lemon juice**
- **1 tablespoon Cajun seasoning**

1. Preheat the air fryer to 400°F.
2. Carefully cut open lobster tails with kitchen scissors and pull back the shell a little to expose the meat. Drizzle butter and lemon juice over each tail, then sprinkle with Cajun seasoning.
3. Place tails in the air fryer basket and cook 10 minutes until lobster shells are bright red and internal temperature reaches at least 145°F. Serve warm.

PER SERVING

CALORIES: 190 | **FAT:** 7g | **PROTEIN:** 28g | **SODIUM:** 1,230mg | **FIBER:** 0g | **CARBOHYDRATES:** 2g | **SUGAR:** 0g

Crab Rangoon

This takeout classic is easy to make in the air fryer. You'll love the brown and crispy wonton wrapper and creamy inside. Every bite is full of deliciously sweet crab flavor.

Pantry Staples: none
Hands-On Time: 10 minutes
Cook Time: 5 minutes

Serves 4

½ cup imitation crabmeat
4 ounces full-fat cream cheese, softened
¼ teaspoon Worcestershire sauce
8 wonton wrappers

IMITATION CRAB

This recipe uses imitation crab, which is often made of multiple types of seafood and processed to look like red and white pieces of crab. This budget-friendly version is usually what you'll find in crab rangoon when you buy them premade. Imitation crab has added sugar to make it slightly sweet like real crab, and it's a great alternative to use for a fraction of the price.

1. Preheat the air fryer to 400°F.
2. In a medium bowl, mix crabmeat, cream cheese, and Worcestershire until combined.
3. Place wonton wrappers on work surface. For each rangoon, scoop ½ tablespoon crab mixture onto center of a wonton wrapper. Press opposing edges toward the center and pinch to close. Spray with cooking spray to coat well. Repeat with remaining crab mixture and wontons.
4. Place in the air fryer basket and cook 5 minutes until brown at the edges. Serve warm.

PER SERVING (SERVING SIZE: 2 RANGOONS)

CALORIES: 150 | **FAT:** 10g | **PROTEIN:** 6g | **SODIUM:** 340mg | **FIBER:** 1g | **CARBOHYDRATES:** 8g | **SUGAR:** 1g

Fish Fillet Sandwich

If you love ultra-crunchy fish sandwiches, you will love this recipe. This meal utilizes cornflakes to get a super-crispy coating on the outside without adding any corn flavor. You'll be surprised at how easy it is to make this fresh-tasting recipe at home.

Pantry Staples: salt, ground black pepper
Hands-On Time: 10 minutes
Cook Time: 18 minutes

Serves 4

4 (3-ounce) cod fillets
½ teaspoon salt
¼ teaspoon ground black pepper
2 cups unsweetened cornflakes, crushed
1 cup Italian bread crumbs
2 large eggs
4 sandwich buns

1. Preheat the air fryer to 375°F.
2. Sprinkle cod with salt and pepper on both sides.
3. In a large bowl, combine cornflakes and bread crumbs.
4. In a medium bowl, whisk eggs. Press each piece of cod into eggs to coat, shaking off excess, then into cornflake mixture to coat evenly on both sides. Spritz with cooking spray.
5. Place in the air fryer basket and cook 18 minutes, turning halfway through cooking time, until fillets are brown and internal temperature reaches at least 145°F. Place on buns to serve.

PER SERVING

CALORIES: 390 | **FAT:** 7g | **PROTEIN:** 28g | **SODIUM:** 1,110mg | **FIBER:** 0g | **CARBOHYDRATES:** 53g | **SUGAR:** 6g

Teriyaki Salmon

There are so many ways to flavor salmon. Teriyaki sauce has a taste similar to soy sauce, but it's sweeter and makes a delicious glaze. This healthy meal would be excellent alongside steamed rice and vegetables for an easy weeknight win.

Pantry Staples: salt
Hands-On Time: 5 minutes
Cook Time: 27 minutes

Serves 4

½ cup teriyaki sauce
¼ teaspoon salt
1 teaspoon ground ginger
½ teaspoon garlic powder
4 (6-ounce) boneless, skinless salmon fillets
2 tablespoons toasted sesame seeds

1. In a large bowl, whisk teriyaki sauce, salt, ginger, and garlic powder. Add salmon to the bowl, being sure to coat each side with marinade. Cover and let marinate in refrigerator 15 minutes.
2. Preheat the air fryer to 375°F.
3. Spritz fillets with cooking spray and place in the air fryer basket. Cook 12 minutes, turning halfway through cooking time, until glaze has caramelized to a dark brown color, salmon flakes easily, and internal temperature reaches at least 145°F. Sprinkle sesame seeds on salmon and serve warm.

PER SERVING

CALORIES: 270 | **FAT:** 9g | **PROTEIN:** 38g | **SODIUM:** 1,660mg | **FIBER:** 0g | **CARBOHYDRATES:** 6g | **SUGAR:** 5g

Shrimp Burgers

These juicy burgers are about to become your new favorite way to enjoy shrimp. While shrimp is usually sautéed or battered, this recipe uses chopped shrimp to make a plump, juicy burger with a flavor all its own. Try enjoying these on toasted buns with chipotle mayonnaise and shredded lettuce for a hearty meal.

Pantry Staples: salt, ground black pepper
Hands-On Time: 10 minutes
Cook Time: 10 minutes

Serves 4

10 ounces medium shrimp, peeled and deveined
¼ cup mayonnaise
½ cup panko bread crumbs
½ teaspoon Old Bay Seasoning
¼ teaspoon salt
⅛ teaspoon ground black pepper
4 hamburger buns

1. Preheat the air fryer to 400°F.
2. In a food processor, add shrimp and pulse four times until broken down.
3. Scoop shrimp into a large bowl and mix with mayonnaise, bread crumbs, Old Bay, salt, and pepper until well combined.
4. Separate mixture into four portions and form into patties. They will feel wet but should be able to hold their shape.
5. Place in the air fryer basket and cook 10 minutes, turning halfway through cooking time, until burgers are brown and internal temperature reaches at least 145°F. Serve warm on buns.

PER SERVING

CALORIES: 300 | **FAT:** 13g | **PROTEIN:** 15g | **SODIUM:** 920mg | **FIBER:** 0g | **CARBOHYDRATES:** 30g | **SUGAR:** 4g

8

Vegetarian Main Dishes

The magic of the air fryer doesn't only extend to meats. Whether you're trying out a Meatless Monday or you're a full fledged vegetarian, this chapter has something for you. With your air fryer, you can cook easy, meat-free, nutrient-dense meals in minutes. And these meals definitely satisfy. From Black Bean Burgers to Chipotle Chickpea Tacos, this chapter will make your meatless dreams come true!

Cheesy Vegetarian Lasagna

This easy, cheesy lasagna is the perfect way to bring a delicious Italian favorite to your next Meatless Monday. Ditch the beef and load up on the cheeses to make a filling and scrumptious meal done entirely in your air fryer!

Pantry Staples: salt, ground black pepper
Hands-On Time: 10 minutes
Cook Time: 40 minutes

Serves 4

- **1¼ cups shredded Italian-blend cheese, divided**
- **½ cup grated vegetarian Parmesan cheese, divided**
- **½ cup full-fat ricotta cheese**
- **½ teaspoon salt**
- **¼ teaspoon ground black pepper**
- **2 cups tomato pasta sauce, divided**
- **5 no-boil lasagna noodles**

OVEN-READY NOODLES

This recipe uses oven-ready or "no boil" noodles, which eliminates the need to cook the noodles in water before using. They're often thinner than traditional lasagna noodles or parboiled, depending on the brand. They cook quickly and use the liquid from the sauce to bake and soften. If you prefer, you can use traditional noodles. Simply boil them on the stove according to package instructions before assembling the lasagna.

1. Preheat the air fryer to 360°F. Spritz a 6" round baking pan with cooking spray.
2. In a medium bowl, mix 1 cup Italian-blend cheese, ¼ cup Parmesan, ricotta, salt, and pepper.
3. Pour ½ cup pasta sauce into the bottom of the prepared pan. Break the noodles into pieces to fit the pan. Place a layer of noodles into the pan.
4. Separate ricotta mixture into three portions. Spread one-third of the mixture over noodles in the pan. Pour ½ cup pasta sauce over ricotta mixture. Repeat layers of noodles, cheese mixture, and pasta sauce twice more until all ingredients are used, topping the final layer with remaining Italian-blend cheese.
5. Cover pan tightly with foil, being sure to tuck foil under the bottom of the pan to ensure the air fryer fan does not blow it off. Place in the air fryer basket. Cook 35 minutes, then remove foil and cook an additional 5 minutes until the top is golden brown and noodles are fork-tender.
6. Remove from the air fryer basket and top with remaining Parmesan and let cool 5 minutes before serving.

PER SERVING

CALORIES: 400 | **FAT:** 19g | **PROTEIN:** 20g | **SODIUM:** 1,400mg | **FIBER:** 0g | **CARBOHYDRATES:** 38g | **SUGAR:** 13g

Sweet and Spicy Barbecue Tofu

Tofu can be an excellent replacement for chicken. But it can also be overwhelming to figure out how to flavor and cook it in a way that's crispy and delicious rather than bland and mushy. By pressing the tofu before cooking it, you'll remove its excess moisture, making for an enjoyable bite every time!

Pantry Staples: salt
Hands-On Time: 10 minutes
Cook Time: 1 hour 15 minutes

Serves 4

- 1 (14-ounce) package extra-firm tofu, drained
- ½ cup barbecue sauce
- ½ cup brown sugar
- 1 teaspoon liquid smoke
- 1 teaspoon crushed red pepper flakes
- ½ teaspoon salt

TOFU PRESS

If you eat tofu frequently, you may want to consider investing in a tofu press. It's a small kitchen gadget that presses the extra moisture out of the tofu without needing paper towels to catch the moisture. You can find one at home stores or online.

1. Press tofu block to remove excess moisture. If you don't have a tofu press, line a baking sheet with paper towels and set tofu on top. Set a second baking sheet on top of tofu and weight it with a heavy item such as a skillet. Let tofu sit at least 30 minutes, changing paper towels if necessary.
2. Cut pressed tofu into twenty-four equal pieces. Set aside.
3. In a large bowl, combine barbecue sauce, brown sugar, liquid smoke, red pepper flakes, and salt. Mix well and add tofu, coating completely. Cover and let marinate at least 30 minutes on the counter.
4. Preheat the air fryer to 400°F.
5. Spray the air fryer basket with cooking spray and add marinated tofu. Cook 15 minutes, shaking the basket twice during cooking.
6. Let cool 10 minutes before serving warm.

PER SERVING

CALORIES: 250 | **FAT:** 5g | **PROTEIN:** 10g | **SODIUM:** 640mg | **FIBER:** 0g | **CARBOHYDRATES:** 42g | **SUGAR:** 37g

Black Bean Burgers

This dish has a flavor all its own and is packed with protein. The ingredients give it a southwest-style flavor and make every bite delicious. Enjoy this burger on a whole-wheat bun with a spoonful of chipotle mayonnaise for a filling and nutritious meal.

Pantry Staples: salt, ground black pepper
Hands-On Time: 10 minutes
Cook Time: 10 minutes

Serves 4

1 (14.5-ounce) can black beans, drained and rinsed
½ cup diced yellow onion
1 medium red bell pepper, seeded and diced
1 large egg
½ cup plain bread crumbs
½ teaspoon salt
¼ teaspoon ground black pepper

1. Preheat the air fryer to 370°F.
2. In a large bowl, add black beans and use a paper towel to pat dry and remove as much excess moisture as possible. Use a fork to mash until beans are mostly broken down.
3. Mix in onion, bell pepper, egg, bread crumbs, salt, and black pepper. Fold until well combined.
4. Separate mixture into four portions, then form each into a patty about ½" thick. Spritz both sides of each patty with cooking spray.
5. Place in the air fryer basket and cook 10 minutes, turning halfway through cooking time, until burgers are firm and hold together. Serve warm.

PER SERVING

CALORIES: 180 | **FAT:** 2g | **PROTEIN:** 11g | **SODIUM:** 510mg | **FIBER:** 1g | **CARBOHYDRATES:** 29g | **SUGAR:** 51g

Black Bean and Rice Burrito Filling

This recipe is a meal prepper's delight. It can make a variety of meals, so your lunch will never feel boring. Add this filling to a large tortilla, scoop it with chips, or even enjoy it as a bowl meal with your favorite toppings.

Pantry Staples: none
Hands-On Time: 5 minutes
Cook Time: 20 minutes

Serves 4

1 cup uncooked instant long-grain white rice
1 cup salsa
½ cup vegetable broth
1 cup black beans
½ cup corn

1. Preheat the air fryer to 400°F.
2. Mix all ingredients in a 3-quart baking dish until well combined.
3. Cover with foil, being sure to tuck foil under the bottom of the pan to ensure the air fryer fan does not blow it off.
4. Cook 20 minutes, stirring twice during cooking. Serve warm.

PER SERVING

CALORIES: 180 | **FAT:** 1g | **PROTEIN:** 7g | **SODIUM:** 530mg | **FIBER:** 6g | **CARBOHYDRATES:** 38g | **SUGAR:** 4g

INSTANT RICE

Instant rice (Minute Rice is a popular brand) is perfect for when you don't have time to cook traditional rice. It cooks in a few minutes and tastes just as good. If you prefer, you can use fully cooked rice in this recipe. Simply eliminate the vegetable broth from the ingredients and reduce the cooking time to 15 minutes.

Roasted Vegetable Grilled Cheese

This restaurant-style grilled cheese will be your new favorite go-to meal. The secret to this delicious sandwich is the white American cheese, which you can often find at the deli. When it melts it becomes ultra-creamy, almost saucelike. It's the perfect complement to the tang and crunch of the bread and plays well with the sweetness of the vegetables. Feel free to add your own favorite vegetables, such as sautéed mushrooms or spinach.

Pantry Staples: none
Hands-On Time: 5 minutes
Cook Time: 6 minutes

Serves 4

- 8 slices sourdough bread
- 4 (1-ounce) slices provolone cheese
- ½ cup chopped roasted red peppers
- ¼ cup chopped yellow onion
- 4 (1-ounce) slices white American cheese

1. Preheat the air fryer to 300°F.
2. Place a slice of bread on a work surface. Top with a slice of provolone, then with 2 tablespoons roasted red peppers and 1 tablespoon onion. Repeat with three more bread slices and remaining provolone and vegetables.
3. Place loaded bread slices in the air fryer basket and cook 1 minute until cheese is melted and onion is softened.
4. Remove the air fryer basket and carefully place 1 slice of American cheese on top of each slice of bread, finishing each with a second slice of bread to complete each sandwich.
5. Spritz the top with cooking spray. Increase the air fryer temperature to 400°F and cook 5 minutes, turning carefully after 3 minutes, until bread is golden and cheese is melted. Serve warm.

PER SERVING

CALORIES: 440 | **FAT:** 20g | **PROTEIN:** 18g | **SODIUM:** 1,300mg | **FIBER:** 0g | **CARBOHYDRATES:** 46g | **SUGAR:** 6g

Twice-Baked Broccoli-Cheddar Potatoes

These potatoes are crispy on the outside and full of gooey goodness on the inside. The soft potato is fluffy and creamy like mashed potatoes. While this dish is entrée worthy, it can also make a tasty side dish with smaller potatoes.

Pantry Staples: salt, ground black pepper
Hands-On Time: 5 minutes
Cook Time: 35 minutes

Serves 4

4 large russet potatoes
2 tablespoons plus 2 teaspoons ranch dressing
1 teaspoon salt
½ teaspoon ground black pepper
¼ cup chopped cooked broccoli florets
1 cup shredded sharp Cheddar cheese

1. Preheat the air fryer to 400°F.
2. Using a fork, poke several holes in potatoes. Place in the air fryer basket and cook 30 minutes until fork-tender.
3. Once potatoes are cool enough to handle, slice lengthwise and scoop out the cooked potato into a large bowl, being careful to maintain the structural integrity of potato skins. Add ranch dressing, salt, pepper, broccoli, and Cheddar to potato flesh and stir until well combined.
4. Scoop potato mixture back into potato skins and return to the air fryer basket. Cook an additional 5 minutes until cheese is melted. Serve warm.

PER SERVING

CALORIES: 320 | **FAT:** 13g | **PROTEIN:** 12g | **SODIUM:** 860mg | **FIBER:** 3g | **CARBOHYDRATES:** 42g | **SUGAR:** 2g

Spinach and Feta Pinwheels

If you love Mediterranean-style flavors, this recipe will be your new go-to appetizer. It's incredibly easy and comes together in less than 30 minutes, making it the perfect last-minute addition to any weeknight meal or even the holiday appetizer plate. The edges become golden brown and fluffy while the cream cheese and feta melt into what makes the perfect delicious bite.

Pantry Staples: salt
Hands-On Time: 10 minutes
Cook Time: 15 minutes

Serves 4

- 1 sheet frozen puff pastry, thawed
- 3 ounces full-fat cream cheese, softened
- 1 (10-ounce) bag frozen spinach, thawed and drained
- ¼ teaspoon salt
- ⅓ cup crumbled feta cheese
- 1 large egg, whisked

1. Preheat the air fryer to 320°F. Unroll puff pastry into a flat rectangle.
2. In a medium bowl, mix cream cheese, spinach, and salt until well combined.
3. Spoon cream cheese mixture onto pastry in an even layer, leaving a ½" border around the edges.
4. Sprinkle feta evenly across dough and gently press into filling to secure. Roll lengthwise to form a log shape.
5. Cut the roll into twelve 1" pieces. Brush with egg. Place in the air fryer basket and cook 15 minutes, turning halfway through cooking time.
6. Let cool 5 minutes before serving.

PER SERVING

CALORIES: 190 | **FAT:** 14g | **PROTEIN:** 8g | **SODIUM:** 450mg | **FIBER:** 2g | **CARBOHYDRATES:** 8g | **SUGAR:** 2g

Layered Ravioli Bake

This dish is perfect for those who love pasta loaded with cheese. This red sauce dish is an easy weeknight meal that's also budget-friendly. Pair with Garlic Knots in Chapter 4 for a complete meal.

Pantry Staples: none
Hands-On Time: 5 minutes
Cook Time: 20 minutes

Serves 4

- 2 cups marinara sauce, divided
- 2 (10-ounce) packages fresh cheese ravioli
- 12 (0.5-ounce) slices provolone cheese
- ½ cup Italian bread crumbs
- ½ cup grated vegetarian Parmesan cheese

1. Preheat the air fryer to 350°F.
2. In the bottom of a 3-quart baking pan, spread ⅓ cup marinara. Place 6 ravioli on top of the sauce, then add 3 slices provolone on top, then another layer of ⅓ cup marinara. Repeat these layers three times to use up remaining ravioli, provolone, and sauce.
3. In a small bowl, mix bread crumbs and Parmesan. Sprinkle over the top of dish.
4. Cover pan with foil, being sure to tuck foil under the bottom of the pan to ensure the air fryer fan does not blow it off. Place pan in the air fryer basket and cook 15 minutes.
5. Remove foil and cook an additional 5 minutes until the top is brown and bubbling. Serve warm.

PER SERVING

CALORIES: 580 | **FAT:** 24g | **PROTEIN:** 32g | **SODIUM:** 1,480mg | **FIBER:** 0g | **CARBOHYDRATES:** 56g | **SUGAR:** 10g

Stuffed Mushrooms

This savory dish has it all—the outside is golden and crispy, the inside is creamy, and each bite is topped off with just a hint of heat.

Pantry Staples: none
Hands-On Time: 10 minutes
Cook Time: 10 minutes

Serves 4

- 12 baby bella mushrooms, stems removed
- 4 ounces full-fat cream cheese, softened
- ¼ cup grated vegetarian Parmesan cheese
- ¼ cup Italian bread crumbs
- 1 teaspoon crushed red pepper flakes

1. Preheat the air fryer to 400°F.
2. Use a spoon to hollow out mushroom caps.
3. In a medium bowl, combine cream cheese, Parmesan, bread crumbs, and red pepper flakes. Scoop approximately 1 tablespoon mixture into each mushroom cap.
4. Place stuffed mushrooms in the air fryer basket and cook 10 minutes until stuffing is brown. Let cool 5 minutes before serving.

PER SERVING

CALORIES: 160 | **FAT:** 11g | **PROTEIN:** 11g | **SODIUM:** 260mg | **FIBER:** 0g | **CARBOHYDRATES:** 9g | **SUGAR:** 2g

Chipotle Chickpea Tacos

Chickpeas, also known as garbanzo beans, are an excellent alternative to meat. They're full of nutrients like magnesium and potassium and are a good source of both protein and fiber. This filling recipe swaps out a typical taco meat for wonderfully seasoned chickpeas to make a recipe even a meat lover would enjoy. The sauce gives them a unique smoky heat that pairs well with fresh ingredients.

Pantry Staples: salt, ground black pepper
Hands-On Time: 10 minutes
Cook Time: 10 minutes

Serves 4

- **2 (15-ounce) cans chickpeas, drained and rinsed**
- **¼ cup adobo sauce**
- **¾ teaspoon salt**
- **¼ teaspoon ground black pepper**
- **8 medium flour tortillas, warmed**
- **1½ cups chopped avocado**
- **½ cup chopped fresh cilantro**

1. Preheat the air fryer to 375°F.
2. In a large bowl, toss chickpeas, adobo, salt, and pepper to fully coat.
3. Using a slotted spoon, place chickpeas in the air fryer basket and cook 10 minutes, shaking the basket twice during cooking, until tender.
4. To assemble, scoop ¼ cup chickpeas into a tortilla, then top with avocado and cilantro. Repeat with remaining tortillas and filling. Serve warm.

PER SERVING

CALORIES: 520 | **FAT:** 16g | **PROTEIN:** 19g | **SODIUM:** 960mg | **FIBER:** 17g | **CARBOHYDRATES:** 79g | **SUGAR:** 9g

ADOBO SAUCE

Adobo sauce is found in the international aisle at the grocery store. It's often labeled as chipotle peppers in adobo sauce. Once you open the can, pour the entire contents into a blender and process until smooth. This will break up the peppers and give you all the flavor.

Pizza Dough

This is the only recipe you'll need for chewy, delicious, and fluffy pizza dough! With just a handful of ingredients, you can make everything from mini pizzas to cheesy garlic bread right in your air fryer. Add your favorite toppings to complete this meal such as mozzarella cheese or chopped vegetables.

Pantry Staples: all-purpose flour, granulated sugar
Hands-On Time: 15 minutes
Cook Time: 1 hour 10 minutes, plus 10 minutes for additional batches

Yields 4 (5") pizzas

2 cups all-purpose flour
1 tablespoon granulated sugar
1 tablespoon quick-rise yeast
4 tablespoons olive oil, divided
¾ cup warm water

1. In a large bowl, mix flour, sugar, and yeast until combined. Add 2 tablespoons oil and warm water and mix until dough becomes smooth.
2. On a lightly floured surface, knead dough 10 minutes, then form into a smooth ball. Drizzle with remaining 2 tablespoons oil, then cover with plastic. Let dough rise 1 hour until doubled in size.
3. Preheat the air fryer to 320°F.
4. Separate dough into four pieces and press each into a 6" pan or air fryer pizza tray that has been spritzed with cooking oil.
5. Add any desired toppings. Place in the air fryer basket, working in batches as necessary, and cook 10 minutes until crust is brown at the edges and toppings are heated through. Serve warm.

PER SERVING (SERVING SIZE: 1 PIZZA)

CALORIES: 360 | **FAT:** 14g | **PROTEIN:** 7g | **SODIUM:** 0mg | **FIBER:** 3g | **CARBOHYDRATES:** 52g | **SUGAR:** 3g

Cheesy Cauliflower Crust Pizza

This recipe is a great way to get an extra helping of vegetables into your day. It's perfect for any of your favorite pizza toppings. If you're new to cauliflower crust, don't worry; the flavor is mild, and it makes a great low-carb alternative.

Pantry Staples: none
Hands-On Time: 10 minutes
Cook Time: 12 minutes per batch

Yields 2 (6") pizzas

- 2 (10-ounce) steamer bags cauliflower florets
- 1 large egg
- 1 cup grated vegetarian Parmesan cheese
- 3 cups shredded mozzarella cheese, divided
- 1 cup pizza sauce

1. Preheat the air fryer to 375°F. Cut two pieces of parchment paper to fit the air fryer basket, one for each crust.
2. Cook cauliflower in the microwave according to package instructions, then drain in a colander. Run under cold water until cool to the touch. Use a cheesecloth to squeeze the excess water from cauliflower, removing as much as possible.
3. In a food processor, combine cauliflower, egg, Parmesan, and 1 cup mozzarella. Process on low about 15 seconds until a sticky ball forms.
4. Separate dough into two pieces. Working with damp hands to prevent dough from sticking, press each dough ball into a 6" round.
5. Place crust on parchment in the air fryer basket, working in batches as necessary. Cook 6 minutes, then flip over with a spatula and top the crust with ½ cup pizza sauce and 1 cup mozzarella. Cook an additional 6 minutes until edges are dark brown and cheese is brown and bubbling. Let cool at least 5 minutes before serving. The crust firms up as it cools.

PER SERVING (SERVING SIZE: 1 PIZZA)

CALORIES: 880 | **FAT:** 51g | **PROTEIN:** 76g | **SODIUM:** 2,290mg | **FIBER:** 5g | **CARBOHYDRATES:** 41g | **SUGAR:** 23g

Cheese and Bean Enchiladas

This budget-friendly meal is tasty and simple. Each enchilada is loaded with cheesy goodness. Feel free to top with a scoop of sour cream to complete this meal.

Pantry Staples: none
Hands-On Time: 10 minutes
Cook Time: 9 minutes

Serves 4

- 1 (15-ounce) can pinto beans, drained and rinsed
- 1½ tablespoons taco seasoning
- 1 cup red enchilada sauce, divided
- 1½ cups shredded Mexican-blend cheese, divided
- 4 fajita-size flour tortillas

1. Preheat the air fryer to 320°F.
2. In a large microwave-safe bowl, microwave beans for 1 minute. Mash half the beans and fold into whole beans. Mix in taco seasoning, ¼ cup enchilada sauce, and 1 cup cheese until well combined.
3. Place ¼ cup bean mixture onto each tortilla. Fold up one end about 1", then roll to close.
4. Place enchiladas into a 3-quart baking pan, pushing together as needed to make them fit. Pour remaining ¾ cup enchilada sauce over enchiladas and top with remaining ½ cup cheese.
5. Place pan in the air fryer basket and cook 8 minutes until cheese is brown and bubbling and the edges of tortillas are brown. Serve warm.

PER SERVING

CALORIES: 370 | **FAT:** 16g | **PROTEIN:** 19g | **SODIUM:** 960mg | **FIBER:** 0g | **CARBOHYDRATES:** 38g | **SUGAR:** 2g

Spaghetti Squash

This base can be used to make lots of delicious recipes. You can enjoy squash with butter or top it with your favorite sauce. You'll need to plan ahead for this one, because it takes 45 minutes to cook, but it reheats easily, making it perfect for meal prep.

Pantry Staples: salt, ground black pepper
Hands-On Time: 5 minutes
Cook Time: 45 minutes

Serves 4

- 1 large spaghetti squash, halved lengthwise and seeded
- 1 teaspoon salt
- ½ teaspoon ground black pepper
- 1 teaspoon garlic powder
- 1 teaspoon dried parsley
- 2 tablespoons salted butter, melted

1. Preheat the air fryer to 350°F.
2. Sprinkle squash with salt, pepper, garlic powder, and parsley. Spritz with cooking spray.
3. Place skin side down in the air fryer basket and cook 30 minutes.
4. Turn squash skin side up and cook an additional 15 minutes until fork-tender. You should be able to easily use a fork to scrape across the surface to separate the strands.
5. Place strands in a medium bowl, top with butter, and toss. Serve warm.

PER SERVING

CALORIES: 290 | **FAT:** 11g | **PROTEIN:** 6g | **SODIUM:** 780mg | **FIBER:** 0g | **CARBOHYDRATES:** 0g | **SUGAR:** 33g

MAKE IT YOUR OWN

This simple recipe is perfect for adding your favorite sauce. Pesto, marinara, and even Alfredo sauce are tasty with spaghetti squash. Use it as you would spaghetti and get creative, adding cheese or even cooked crumbled tofu.

Toasted Ravioli

Traditional ravioli is soft and covered in sauce, but this dish gives your meal a crunchy upgrade that even picky eaters will enjoy. The golden brown edges are the perfect first bite followed by a creamy, cheese-filled inside. Feel free to add a sprinkle of vegetarian Parmesan on top and a pinch of parsley for a restaurant-style presentation.

Pantry Staples: none
Hands-On Time: 10 minutes
Cook Time: 8 minutes

Serves 4

- 1 cup Italian bread crumbs
- 2 tablespoons grated vegetarian Parmesan cheese
- 1 large egg
- ¼ cup whole milk
- 1 (10-ounce) package fresh cheese ravioli

1. Preheat the air fryer to 400°F.
2. In a large bowl, whisk together bread crumbs and Parmesan.
3. In a medium bowl, whisk together egg and milk.
4. Dip each ravioli into egg mixture, shaking off the excess, then press into bread crumb mixture until well coated. Spritz each side with cooking spray.
5. Place in the air fryer basket and cook 8 minutes, turning halfway through cooking time, until ravioli is brown at the edges and crispy. Serve warm.

PER SERVING

CALORIES: 290 | **FAT:** 8g | **PROTEIN:** 15g | **SODIUM:** 670mg | **FIBER:** 0g | **CARBOHYDRATES:** 38g | **SUGAR:** 4g

Spicy Corn Fritters

This dish is surprisingly filling and a great addition to your menu lineup. This extra-large spicy fritter gets crispy and delicious in around 20 minutes. This meal would be extra-tasty with a spoonful of sour cream and topped with sliced green onions.

Pantry Staples: all-purpose flour, salt, ground black pepper
Hands-On Time: 10 minutes
Cook Time: 22 minutes

Serves 4

1 (15.25-ounce) can yellow corn, drained
½ cup all-purpose flour
¾ cup shredded pepper jack cheese
1 large egg
½ teaspoon chili powder
¼ teaspoon garlic powder
½ teaspoon salt
¼ teaspoon ground black pepper

1. Cut parchment paper to fit the air fryer basket.
2. In a large bowl, mix all ingredients until well combined. Using a ½-cup scoop, separate mixture into four portions.
3. Gently press each into a 4" round and spritz with cooking spray. Place in freezer 10 minutes.
4. Preheat the air fryer to 400°F.
5. Place fritters in the air fryer basket and cook 12 minutes, turning halfway through cooking time, until fritters are brown on the top and edges and firm to the touch. Serve warm.

PER SERVING

CALORIES: 230 | **FAT:** 9g | **PROTEIN:** 10g | **SODIUM:** 450mg | **FIBER:** 4g | **CARBOHYDRATES:** 32g | **SUGAR:** 8g

Pesto Vegetable Kebabs

This flavorful entrée is sure to delight basil lovers. Pesto is the perfect sauce for vegetables because it's made of fresh herbs and oil, both of which help keep moisture and flavor in your food. This recipe is perfect on its own or with a bowl of steamed rice.

Pantry Staples: salt, ground black pepper
Hands-On Time: 10 minutes
Cook Time: 8 minutes

Serves 4

- 12 ounces button mushrooms
- 12 ounces cherry tomatoes
- 2 medium zucchini, cut into ¼" slices
- 1 medium red onion, peeled and cut into 1" cubes
- 1 cup pesto, divided
- ½ teaspoon salt
- ¼ teaspoon ground black pepper

1. Soak eight 6" skewers in water 10 minutes to avoid burning. Preheat the air fryer to 350°F.
2. Place a mushroom on a skewer, followed by a tomato, zucchini slice, and red onion piece. Repeat to fill up the skewer, then follow the same pattern for remaining skewers.
3. Brush each skewer evenly using ½ cup pesto. Sprinkle kebabs with salt and pepper. Place in the air fryer basket and cook 10 minutes, turning halfway through cooking time, until vegetables are tender. Brush kebabs with remaining ½ cup pesto before serving.

PER SERVING (SERVING SIZE: 3 KEBABS)

CALORIES: 330 | **FAT:** 27g | **PROTEIN:** 8g | **SODIUM:** 910mg | **FIBER:** 4g | **CARBOHYDRATES:** 17g | **SUGAR:** 8g

ADD YOUR FAVORITE VEGETABLES

This recipe works great with just about any vegetables as long as they're cut to a similar size. Any type of squash, pepper, or even mini par-baked potatoes makes a great addition. You can assemble these in the morning, and they will still be fresh for cooking at dinnertime.

Portobello Mini Pizzas

Mushrooms are loaded with nutrients and also have a great umami flavor. These pizzas are savory and filling and great for any meal. Feel free to add your own spin to these pizzas using your favorite toppings.

Pantry Staples: salt, ground black pepper
Hands-On Time: 5 minutes
Cook Time: 10 minutes

Serves 4

- 4 large portobello mushrooms, stems removed
- 2 cups shredded mozzarella cheese, divided
- ½ cup full-fat ricotta cheese
- 1 teaspoon salt, divided
- ½ teaspoon ground black pepper
- 1 teaspoon Italian seasoning
- 1 cup pizza sauce

1. Preheat the air fryer to 350°F.
2. Use a spoon to hollow out mushroom caps. Spritz mushrooms with cooking spray. Place ¼ cup mozzarella into each mushroom cap.
3. In a small bowl, mix ricotta, ½ teaspoon salt, pepper, and Italian seasoning. Divide mixture evenly and spoon into mushroom caps (about 1 tablespoon for each).
4. Pour ¼ cup pizza sauce into each mushroom cap, then top each with ¼ cup mozzarella. Sprinkle tops of pizzas with remaining salt.
5. Place mushrooms in the air fryer basket and cook 10 minutes until cheese is brown and bubbling. Serve warm.

PER SERVING

CALORIES: 290 | **FAT:** 16g | **PROTEIN:** 24g | **SODIUM:** 1,310mg | **FIBER:** 1g | **CARBOHYDRATES:** 17g | **SUGAR:** 10g

Spinach Pesto Flatbread

This flavorful meal is the perfect lunch for busy days. It uses fresh mozzarella for that delicious stringy melted cheese we all love. If you've never purchased fresh mozzarella before, look for it in the cheese section of your grocery store or by the deli. It's available in a ball or log shape.

Pantry Staples: none
Hands-On Time: 5 minutes
Cook Time: 8 minutes per batch

Serves 4

- 1 cup basil pesto
- 4 (6") round flatbreads
- ½ cup chopped frozen spinach, thawed and drained
- 8 ounces fresh mozzarella cheese, sliced
- 1 teaspoon crushed red pepper flakes

1. Preheat the air fryer to 350°F.
2. For each flatbread, spread ¼ cup pesto across flatbread, then scatter 2 tablespoons spinach over pesto. Top with 2 ounces mozzarella slices and ¼ teaspoon red pepper flakes. Repeat with remaining flatbread and toppings.
3. Place in the air fryer basket, working in batches as necessary, and cook 8 minutes until cheese is brown and bubbling. Serve warm.

PER SERVING

CALORIES: 720 | **FAT:** 47g | **PROTEIN:** 31g | **SODIUM:** 1,270mg | **FIBER:** 1g | **CARBOHYDRATES:** 49g | **SUGAR:** 3g

Caprese Eggplant Stacks

There are many great ways to enjoy eggplant, and this stack is a fun twist on caprese flavor, full of gooey fresh mozzarella and topped with aromatic basil. If you enjoy a little acidity, try topping with a drizzle of balsamic vinegar.

Pantry Staples: salt, ground black pepper
Hands-On Time: 10 minutes
Cook Time: 8 minutes

Serves 4

- 1 medium eggplant, cut into 4 (½") slices
- ½ teaspoon salt
- ¼ teaspoon ground black pepper
- 4 (¼") slices tomato
- 2 ounces fresh mozzarella cheese, cut into 4 slices
- 1 tablespoon olive oil
- ¼ cup fresh basil, sliced

1. Preheat the air fryer to 320°F.
2. In a 6" round pan, place eggplant slices. Sprinkle with salt and pepper. Top each with a tomato slice, then a mozzarella slice, and drizzle with oil.
3. Place in the air fryer basket and cook 8 minutes until eggplant is tender and cheese is melted. Garnish with fresh basil to serve.

PER SERVING

CALORIES: 110 | **FAT:** 6g | **PROTEIN:** 5g | **SODIUM:** 390mg | **FIBER:** 3g | **CARBOHYDRATES:** 8g | **SUGAR:** 4g

Vegetable Nuggets

These golden nuggets are a healthy and delicious meal for lunch or dinner! They're loaded with vegetables and perfect for dipping in ranch dressing.

Pantry Staples: salt, ground black pepper
Hands-On Time: 10 minutes
Cook Time: 10 minutes per batch

Serves 6

- 1 cup shredded carrots
- 2 cups broccoli florets
- 2 large eggs
- 1 cup shredded Cheddar cheese
- 1 cup Italian bread crumbs
- 1 teaspoon salt
- ½ teaspoon ground black pepper

1. Preheat the air fryer to 400°F.
2. In a food processor, combine carrots and broccoli and pulse five times. Add eggs, Cheddar, bread crumbs, salt, and pepper, and pulse ten times.
3. Carefully scoop twenty-four balls, about 1 heaping tablespoon each, out of the mixture. Spritz balls with cooking spray.
4. Place balls in the air fryer basket, working in batches as necessary, and cook 10 minutes, shaking the basket twice during cooking to ensure even browning. Serve warm.

PER SERVING (SERVING SIZE: 4 NUGGETS)

CALORIES: 180 | **FAT:** 9g | **PROTEIN:** 10g | **SODIUM:** 830mg | **FIBER:** 1g | **CARBOHYDRATES:** 16g | **SUGAR:** 2g

9

Desserts

If you have a sweet tooth, you can appreciate the importance of ease and speed when it comes to making a dessert recipe. And thanks to the way air fryers circulate hot air, desserts cook in practically no time. This chapter is full of easy, quick recipes to satisfy your taste buds with perfectly portioned goodies when you need them the most. From classic Chocolate Chip Cookies to Vanilla Cheesecake, there's no shortage of recipes for every craving.

Molten Lava Cakes

Chocoholics rejoice! These decadent lava cakes, complete with a warm, gooey center, cook in just minutes right in your air fryer. Pair them with a scoop of vanilla ice cream to take this indulgent treat to the next level.

Pantry Staples: vanilla extract, salt, all-purpose flour
Hands-On Time: 10 minutes
Cook Time: 10 minutes

Serves 3

- **2 large eggs**
- **1 teaspoon vanilla extract**
- **¼ teaspoon salt**
- **3 tablespoons unsalted butter**
- **¾ cup milk chocolate chips**
- **¼ cup all-purpose flour**

1. Preheat the air fryer to 350°F. Spray three 4" ramekins with cooking spray.
2. In a medium bowl, whisk eggs, vanilla, and salt until well combined.
3. In a large microwave-safe bowl, microwave butter and chocolate chips in 20-second intervals, stirring after each interval, until mixture is fully melted, smooth, and pourable.
4. Whisk chocolate and slowly add egg mixture. Whisk until fully combined.
5. Sprinkle flour into bowl and whisk into chocolate mixture. It should be easily pourable.
6. Divide batter evenly among prepared ramekins. Place in the air fryer basket and cook 5 minutes until the edges and top are set.
7. Let cool 5 minutes and use a butter knife to loosen the edges from ramekins.
8. To serve, place a small dessert plate upside down on top of each ramekin. Quickly flip ramekin and plate upside down so lava cake drops to the plate. Let cool 5 minutes. Serve.

PER SERVING

CALORIES: 410 | **FAT:** 27g | **PROTEIN:** 9g | **SODIUM:** 280mg | **FIBER:** 2g | **CARBOHYDRATES:** 33g | **SUGAR:** 33g

Cinnamon-Sugar Pretzel Bites

These bites are a delicious dessert and a great on-the-go snack. They might remind you of the mall pretzels you loved as a kid. Each crispy bite is full of sweet cinnamon taste on the outside with fluffy pretzel bread in the middle. If you love dipping your pretzel in glaze, you can whip one up by whisking ½ cup confectioners' sugar with 3 tablespoons milk.

Pantry Staples: all-purpose flour, granulated sugar, salt
Hands-On Time: 15 minutes
Cook Time: 1 hour 10 minutes

Serves 4

1 cup all-purpose flour
1 teaspoon quick-rise yeast
2 tablespoons granulated sugar, divided
¼ teaspoon salt
1 tablespoon olive oil
⅓ cup warm water
2 teaspoons baking soda
1 teaspoon ground cinnamon

SHORT ON TIME?

If you don't have the time to make this from scratch, you can use refrigerated pizza dough. Preheat your air fryer to 400°F, then skip down to step 5 and begin there with your premade dough.

1. In a large bowl, mix flour, yeast, 2 teaspoons sugar, and salt until combined.
2. Pour in oil and water and stir until a dough begins to form and pull away from the edges of the bowl. Remove dough from the bowl and transfer to a lightly floured surface. Knead 10 minutes until dough is mostly smooth.
3. Spritz dough with cooking spray and place into a large clean bowl. Cover with plastic wrap and let rise 1 hour.
4. Preheat the air fryer to 400°F.
5. Press dough into a 6" × 4" rectangle. Cut dough into twenty-four even pieces.
6. Fill a medium saucepan over medium-high heat halfway with water and bring to a boil. Add baking soda and let it boil 1 minute, then add pretzel bites. You may need to work in batches. Cook 45 seconds, then remove from water and drain. They will be puffy but should have mostly maintained their shape.
7. Spritz pretzel bites with cooking spray. Place in the air fryer basket and cook 5 minutes until golden brown.
8. In a small bowl, mix remaining sugar and cinnamon. When pretzel bites are done cooking, immediately toss in cinnamon and sugar mixture and serve.

PER SERVING (SERVING SIZE: 6 BITES)

CALORIES: 170 | **FAT:** 3.5g | **PROTEIN:** 3g | **SODIUM:** 780mg | **FIBER:** 2g | **CARBOHYDRATES:** 31g | **SUGAR:** 6g

Brownies

These fudgy, gooey Brownies are the perfect dessert for any chocolate lover! Traditional oven-baked brownies can take more than 45 minutes to bake, but with this recipe and your air fryer, you're just about 20 minutes away from brownie delight!

Pantry Staples: all-purpose flour, granulated sugar, baking powder
Hands-On Time: 5 minutes
Cook Time: 20 minutes

Serves 8

- ½ cup all-purpose flour
- 1 cup granulated sugar
- ¼ cup cocoa powder
- ½ teaspoon baking powder
- 6 tablespoons salted butter, melted
- 1 large egg
- ½ cup semisweet chocolate chips

PAN SIZE

Be sure to use the recommended cake pan size in this recipe or you may end up with over- or undercooked brownies. When you change cooking pan sizes, you'll need to keep watch and determine when your brownies are ready based on visual cues. You may find they need a few more or less minutes to cook.

1. Preheat the air fryer to 350°F. Generously grease two 6" round cake pans.
2. In a large bowl, combine flour, sugar, cocoa powder, and baking powder.
3. Add butter, egg, and chocolate chips to dry ingredients. Stir until well combined.
4. Divide batter between prepared pans. Place in the air fryer basket and cook 20 minutes until a toothpick inserted into the center comes out clean. Cool 5 minutes before serving.

PER SERVING

CALORIES: 270 | **FAT:** 13g | **PROTEIN:** 3g | **SODIUM:** 80mg | **FIBER:** 2g | **CARBOHYDRATES:** 39g | **SUGAR:** 31g

Glazed Chocolate Doughnut Holes

Doughnuts are perfect for both dessert and breakfast. This recipe comes together so quickly, you don't need to plan ahead to make it. The outer layer is crunchy while the inside is chocolatey and fluffy. The glaze gives these doughnut holes the perfect amount of sweetness in every bite. This delicious dessert is sure to earn a spot on your weekly rotation.

Pantry Staples: granulated sugar, vanilla extract
Hands-On Time: 10 minutes
Cook Time: 22 minutes

Serves 5

- **1 cup self-rising flour**
- **1¼ cups plain full-fat Greek yogurt**
- **¼ cup cocoa powder**
- **½ cup granulated sugar**
- **1 cup confectioners' sugar**
- **¼ cup heavy cream**
- **1 teaspoon vanilla extract**

1. Preheat the air fryer to 350°F. Spray the inside of the air fryer basket with cooking spray.
2. In a large bowl, combine flour, yogurt, cocoa powder, and granulated sugar. Knead by hand 5 minutes until a large, sticky ball of dough is formed.
3. Roll mixture into balls, about 2 tablespoons each, to make twenty doughnut holes. Place doughnut holes in the air fryer basket and cook 12 minutes, working in batches as necessary.
4. While doughnut holes are cooking, in a medium bowl, mix confectioners' sugar, cream, and vanilla. Allow doughnut holes 5 minutes to cool before rolling each in the glaze. Chill in the refrigerator 5 minutes to allow glaze to set before serving.

PER SERVING (SERVING SIZE: 4 DOUGHNUTS)

CALORIES: 380 | **FAT:** 9g | **PROTEIN:** 10g | **SODIUM:** 340mg | **FIBER:** 2g | **CARBOHYDRATES:** 67g | **SUGAR:** 47g

Lemon Bars

The bright lemon flavor and sweet filling make these mouthwatering bars everyone's favorite. The golden crunch of the crust gives every bite balance. This recipe calls for lemon juice and while fresh lemons provide the best flavor, bottled lemon juice will still make a delicious dessert.

Pantry Staples: granulated sugar, vanilla extract, all-purpose flour
Hands-On Time: 10 minutes
Cook Time: 20 minutes

Serves 8

- **6 tablespoons salted butter, softened**
- **¾ cup granulated sugar, divided**
- **1 teaspoon vanilla extract**
- **1 cup plus 2 tablespoons all-purpose flour, divided**
- **¼ cup lemon juice**
- **2 large eggs**
- **1 teaspoon lemon zest**

1. Preheat the air fryer to 350°F. Spray a 6" round cake pan with cooking spray.
2. In a large bowl, cream together butter and ¼ cup sugar.
3. Stir in vanilla and 1 cup flour. Press this mixture into prepared pan and place in the air fryer basket. Cook 5 minutes until golden brown.
4. In a separate bowl, mix remaining ½ cup sugar, lemon juice, eggs, remaining 2 tablespoons flour, and lemon zest. Pour mixture over baked crust and return to the air fryer to cook for 15 minutes.
5. Let cool completely before cutting into eight sections and serving.

PER SERVING (SERVING SIZE: 1 BAR)

CALORIES: 230 | **FAT:** 10g | **PROTEIN:** 3g | **SODIUM:** 85mg | **FIBER:** 1g | **CARBOHYDRATES:** 33g | **SUGAR:** 19g

Monkey Bread

This sweet and gooey pull-apart bread is the perfect dessert to share. It's best cooked in a Bundt pan to ensure even cooking in the center, but if you don't have a Bundt pan that fits your air fryer, just keep a close eye on the food in a regular 6" cake pan.

Pantry Staples: granulated sugar
Hands-On Time: 5 minutes
Cook Time: 20 minutes

Serves 6

- **1 (16.3-ounce) can refrigerated biscuit dough**
- **½ cup granulated sugar**
- **1 tablespoon ground cinnamon**
- **¼ cup salted butter, melted**
- **¼ cup brown sugar**

1. Preheat the air fryer to 325°F. Spray a 6" round cake pan with cooking spray. Separate biscuits and cut each into four pieces.
2. In a large bowl, stir granulated sugar with cinnamon. Toss biscuit pieces in the cinnamon and sugar mixture until well coated. Place each biscuit piece in prepared pan.
3. In a medium bowl, stir together butter and brown sugar. Pour mixture evenly over the biscuit pieces.
4. Place pan in the air fryer basket and cook 20 minutes until brown. Let cool 10 minutes before flipping bread out of the pan and serving.

PER SERVING

CALORIES: 350 | **FAT:** 10g | **PROTEIN:** 5g | **SODIUM:** 710mg | **FIBER:** 1g | **CARBOHYDRATES:** 62g | **SUGAR:** 29g

Chocolate Chip Cookies

Who doesn't love freshly baked, gooey Chocolate Chip Cookies? They're a quick family classic you'll find yourself making all the time. The edges rise to be chewy and golden while the inside is fluffy and soft.

Pantry Staples: all-purpose flour, baking powder, vanilla extract
Hands-On Time: 5 minutes
Cook Time: 20 minutes

Serves 12

- ½ cup salted butter, melted
- ½ cup brown sugar
- 1 cup all-purpose flour
- 1 large egg
- 1 teaspoon baking powder
- 1 teaspoon vanilla extract
- ⅓ cup semisweet chocolate chips

1. In a large bowl, stir butter, brown sugar, flour, egg, baking powder, and vanilla until well combined.
2. Gently fold in chocolate chips. Chill dough in refrigerator 10 minutes.
3. Preheat the air fryer to 350°F. Cut parchment paper to fit the air fryer basket.
4. Scoop the batter into portions to make twelve 2" balls. Place on parchment paper in the air fryer basket 2" apart and cook 10 minutes until golden brown on the edges and bottom. Serve warm.

PER SERVING (SERVING SIZE: 1 COOKIE)

CALORIES: 170 | **FAT:** 9g | **PROTEIN:** 2g | **SODIUM:** 65mg | **FIBER:** 1g | **CARBOHYDRATES:** 19g | **SUGAR:** 11g

Peanut Butter Cookies

The best peanut butter cookies are dense and full of flavor. These cookies are a peanut butter lover's dream. The crispy edges and moist, soft centers are full of peanut flavor that will keep you reaching for more. For those who like a little crunch, feel free to substitute crunchy peanut butter.

Pantry Staples: all-purpose flour, baking powder
Hands-On Time: 10 minutes
Cook Time: 10 minutes per batch

Serves 9

1 cup creamy peanut butter
1 cup brown sugar
½ cup unsalted butter, melted
2 large eggs
2 cups all-purpose flour
1½ teaspoons baking powder

1. Preheat the air fryer to 325°F. Cut two pieces of parchment paper to fit the air fryer basket, one for each batch.
2. In a large bowl, mix peanut butter and brown sugar until combined.
3. Add butter and eggs, stirring until smooth.
4. In a medium bowl, mix flour and baking powder. Slowly add flour mixture, about a third at a time, to peanut butter mixture. Fold in to combine.
5. Roll dough into balls, about 2 tablespoons each, to make eighteen balls.
6. Place on parchment 2" apart in the air fryer, working in batches as necessary, and cook 10 minutes until the edges are golden brown. Let cool 5 minutes before serving.

PER SERVING (SERVING SIZE: 2 COOKIES)

CALORIES: 480 | **FAT:** 26g | **PROTEIN:** 10g | **SODIUM:** 110mg | **FIBER:** 3g | **CARBOHYDRATES:** 49g | **SUGAR:** 23g

Snickerdoodles

These delightfully sweet cookies will win you over. The cinnamon coating gives them a light but delicious flavor. Their golden edges and chewy centers will be heaven for any cookie lover.

Pantry Staples: granulated sugar, all-purpose flour, baking powder
Hands-On Time: 10 minutes
Cook Time: 10 minutes per batch

Serves 18

½ cup unsalted butter, melted
3 tablespoons granulated sugar, divided
1 cup all-purpose flour
½ teaspoon baking powder
½ teaspoon cream of tartar
1 teaspoon ground cinnamon

1. Preheat the air fryer to 325°F. Cut four pieces of parchment to fit the air fryer basket, one for each batch.
2. In a medium bowl, mix butter and 2 tablespoons sugar.
3. In a large bowl, mix flour, baking powder, and cream of tartar. Add butter mixture to dry ingredients and stir to form dough.
4. Roll dough into balls, about 2 tablespoons each, to make eighteen balls.
5. In a small bowl, mix remaining 1 tablespoon sugar and cinnamon. Roll each ball in sugar mixture.
6. Place on parchment in the air fryer basket 2" apart and cook 10 minutes per batch until the edges are golden brown and a toothpick inserted into the center comes out clean. Let cool 5 minutes before serving.

PER SERVING (SERVING SIZE: 1 COOKIE)

CALORIES: 80 | **FAT:** 5g | **PROTEIN:** 1g | **SODIUM:** 0mg | **FIBER:** 0g | **CARBOHYDRATES:** 8g | **SUGAR:** 2g

Almond Shortbread Cookies

This is one of the easiest cookies you'll ever make. Buttery, delicious, and perfect for the holiday season, once you start eating these shortbread cookies, it will be hard to put them down!

Pantry Staples: granulated sugar, vanilla extract, all-purpose flour
Hands-On Time: 10 minutes
Cook Time: 1 hour 10 minutes

Serves 8

½ cup salted butter, softened
¼ cup granulated sugar
1 teaspoon almond extract
1 teaspoon vanilla extract
2 cups all-purpose flour

1. In a large bowl, cream butter, sugar, and extracts. Gradually add flour, mixing until well combined.
2. Roll dough into a 12" x 2" log and wrap in plastic. Chill in refrigerator at least 1 hour.
3. Preheat the air fryer to 300°F.
4. Slice dough into ¼"-thick cookies. Place in the air fryer basket 2" apart, working in batches as needed, and cook 10 minutes until the edges start to brown. Let cool completely before serving.

PER SERVING (SERVING SIZE: 2 COOKIES)

CALORIES: 240 | **FAT:** 12g | **PROTEIN:** 3g | **SODIUM:** 90mg | **FIBER:** 1g | **CARBOHYDRATES:** 30g | **SUGAR:** 6g

Peach Crumble

This dessert is the perfect summer treat and couldn't be easier to put together. It has soft, delicate peaches and a crispy topping. Try it warm with a scoop of vanilla ice cream for a delicious flavor pairing.

Pantry Staples: all-purpose flour, salt
Hands-On Time: 10 minutes
Cook Time: 10 minutes

Serves 6

½ cup all-purpose flour
¼ cup quick-cooking oats
4 tablespoons cold salted butter, cubed
¼ teaspoon salt
2 teaspoons ground cinnamon, divided
⅓ cup brown sugar, divided
1 (14.6-ounce) can peaches, drained and rinsed

1. Preheat the air fryer to 350°F.
2. In a food processor, place flour, oats, butter, salt, 1 teaspoon cinnamon, and 3 tablespoons brown sugar. Pulse fifteen times until large crumbs form.
3. Place peaches in a 6" round baking dish and sprinkle with remaining cinnamon and brown sugar. Stir to coat peaches.
4. Spoon flour mixture over peaches to cover completely, leaving larger crumbs intact as much as possible. Spritz with cooking spray.
5. Place in the air fryer basket and cook 10 minutes until the top is golden brown. Serve warm.

PER SERVING

CALORIES: 210 | **FAT:** 8g | **PROTEIN:** 2g | **SODIUM:** 160mg | **FIBER:** 2g | **CARBOHYDRATES:** 36g | **SUGAR:** 24g

Vanilla Cheesecake

Air fryer cheesecake is so much faster and easier than a traditional oven-baked version, and it's just as delicious! This creamy and flavorful cheesecake comes complete with a graham cracker crust. Serve with a dollop of whipped cream for the perfect finishing touch!

Pantry Staples: granulated sugar, vanilla extract
Hands-On Time: 10 minutes
Cook Time: 4 hours 20 minutes

Serves 8

6 full graham cracker sheets
2 tablespoons salted butter, melted
12 ounces full-fat cream cheese, softened
½ cup granulated sugar
2 tablespoons sour cream
1 teaspoon vanilla extract
1 large egg

1. Preheat the air fryer to 300°F.
2. In a food processor, place graham crackers and pulse fifteen times until finely crushed. Transfer crumbs to a medium bowl. You'll have about ½ cup.
3. Add butter and mix until the texture is sand-like. Press into a 6" round springform pan.
4. In a large bowl, combine cream cheese and sugar, stirring until no lumps remain. Mix in sour cream and vanilla until smooth. Gently mix in egg.
5. Pour batter over crust in pan. Place in the air fryer basket and cook 20 minutes until top is golden brown.
6. Chill cheesecake in refrigerator at least 4 hours to set before serving.

PER SERVING

CALORIES: 270 | **FAT:** 19g | **PROTEIN:** 4g | **SODIUM:** 200mg | **FIBER:** 0g | **CARBOHYDRATES:** 20g | **SUGAR:** 16g

PREVENT OVERBROWNING

Some air fryers have more forceful heat fans, which may cause the cheesecake to prematurely brown on top. Keep an eye on things, and if the top is getting too dark, cover it with foil, being sure to tuck foil under the bottom of the pan to ensure the air fryer fan doesn't blow it off.

Crustless Chocolate Cheesecake

This cheesecake is so decadent that you won't even miss the crust, and the filling is as smooth and creamy as fudge. The trick is using cocoa powder and chocolate chips to give it a deep chocolate taste. Add some chocolate shavings on top or a bit of whipped cream when serving for a treat so delicious you won't believe it was made in the air fryer.

Pantry Staples: granulated sugar, vanilla extract
Hands-On Time: 10 minutes
Cook Time: 4 hours 20 minutes

Serves 8

12 ounces full-fat cream cheese, softened
½ cup granulated sugar
2 tablespoons sour cream
2 tablespoons cocoa powder
½ cup semisweet chocolate chips, melted
1 teaspoon vanilla extract
1 large egg

1. Preheat the air fryer to 300°F. Line a 6" round cake pan with parchment paper and spray with cooking spray.
2. In a large bowl, combine cream cheese and sugar until no lumps remain. Mix in sour cream, cocoa powder, chocolate chips, and vanilla until well combined and smooth. Stir in egg. Pour into prepared pan.
3. Place in the air fryer basket and cook 20 minutes until the top of cheesecake is firm.
4. Chill cheesecake in refrigerator at least 4 hours to set before serving.

PER SERVING

CALORIES: 270 | **FAT:** 19g | **PROTEIN:** 4g | **SODIUM:** 150mg | **FIBER:** 1g | **CARBOHYDRATES:** 22g | **SUGAR:** 20g

ADD A CRUST

If you're not a fan of crustless cheesecake, feel free to add your favorite premade crust. You can use a cookie crust or a chocolate graham cracker crust to add another element of texture to this creamy dessert.

Cream Cheese Pound Cake

Pound cakes are a versatile staple dessert and now they're even easier to make in the air fryer. This cake has all the classic flavors and cooks in half the time compared to the oven. Feel free to make it your own by adding your favorite flavor extracts or serving it with fresh berries and whipped cream.

Pantry Staples: all-purpose flour, baking powder, granulated sugar, vanilla extract
Hands-On Time: 10 minutes
Cook Time: 25 minutes

Serves 8

1½ cups all-purpose flour
1 teaspoon baking powder
½ cup salted butter, melted
4 ounces full-fat cream cheese, softened
1 cup granulated sugar
2 teaspoons vanilla extract
3 large eggs

1. Preheat the air fryer to 300°F. Spray a 6" round cake pan with cooking spray.
2. In a large bowl, combine flour and baking powder. In a separate large bowl, mix butter, cream cheese, sugar, and vanilla.
3. Stir wet ingredients into dry ingredients and add eggs one at a time, making sure each egg is fully incorporated before adding the next.
4. Pour batter into prepared pan. Place in the air fryer basket and cook 25 minutes until a toothpick inserted into the center comes out clean. If cake begins to brown too quickly, cover pan with foil and cut two slits in the top of foil to encourage heat circulation. Be sure to tuck foil under the bottom of the pan to ensure the air fryer fan does not blow it off.
5. Allow cake to cool completely before serving.

PER SERVING

CALORIES: 360 | **FAT:** 18g | **PROTEIN:** 6g | **SODIUM:** 100mg | **FIBER:** 1g | **CARBOHYDRATES:** 44g | **SUGAR:** 26g

Apple Fritters

If you're a fan of apple-cinnamon flavor, you'll love this easy dessert. The crunchy edges and soft inside filled with fresh apple pieces will satisfy your cravings for a sweet treat. If you enjoy your fritters with a glaze, mix 1 cup confectioners' sugar with 2 tablespoons milk, then drizzle fritters once they've cooled.

Pantry Staples: granulated sugar
Hands-On Time: 10 minutes
Cook Time: 15 minutes

Serves 6

1 cup self-rising flour
½ cup granulated sugar
1½ teaspoons ground cinnamon
¼ cup whole milk
1 large egg
1 cup diced Granny Smith apples

DON'T HAVE SELF-RISING FLOUR?

Not a problem! You can make your own self-rising flour by mixing together 1 cup all-purpose flour, ½ teaspoon salt, and ½ tablespoon baking powder.

1. Preheat the air fryer to 375°F. Cut parchment paper to fit the air fryer basket.
2. In a large bowl, combine flour, sugar, cinnamon, and milk.
3. Stir in egg and gently fold in apples.
4. Scoop dough in ¼-cup portions onto parchment paper. Place in the air fryer basket and cook 15 minutes, turning halfway through cooking time, until golden brown and a toothpick inserted into the center comes out clean. Let cool 5 minutes before serving.

PER SERVING

CALORIES: 160 | **FAT:** 1g | **PROTEIN:** 3g | **SODIUM:** 280mg | **FIBER:** 1g | **CARBOHYDRATES:** 34g | **SUGAR:** 18g

Pumpkin Pie

Now your favorite fall dessert is a snap to bake! The premade pie mix has all the sugar and spice you need, which makes this recipe easier than ever. You won't be able to tell it wasn't made completely from scratch.

Pantry Staples: vanilla extract
Hands-On Time: 5 minutes
Cook Time: 2 hours 25 minutes

Serves 6

1 (15-ounce) can pumpkin pie mix
1 large egg
1 teaspoon vanilla extract
⅓ cup sweetened condensed milk
1 (6-ounce) premade graham cracker piecrust

1. Preheat the air fryer to 325°F.
2. In a large bowl, whisk together pumpkin pie mix, egg, vanilla, and sweetened condensed milk until well combined. Pour mixture into piecrust.
3. Place in the air fryer basket and cook 25 minutes until pie is brown, firm, and a toothpick inserted into the center comes out clean.
4. Chill in the refrigerator until set, at least 2 hours, before serving.

PER SERVING

CALORIES: 270 | **FAT:** 9g | **PROTEIN:** 4g | **SODIUM:** 280mg | **FIBER:** 0g | **CARBOHYDRATES:** 44g | **SUGAR:** 35g

Peanut Snowball Cookies

This recipe is a twist on the popular wintertime favorite. Snowball cookies are traditionally made with pecans or walnuts, but using chopped peanuts gives a delicious flavor and increases the satisfying crunch in every bite.

Pantry Staples: granulated sugar, vanilla extract, all-purpose flour
Hands-On Time: 10 minutes
Cook Time: 15 minutes per batch

Serves 8

- ½ cup salted butter, melted
- ¼ cup granulated sugar
- 1 teaspoon vanilla extract
- 1 cup all-purpose flour
- 1 cup peanuts, finely chopped
- 2 cups confectioners' sugar

1. Preheat the air fryer to 300°F.
2. In a large bowl, mix butter, sugar, and vanilla. Gradually add flour and peanuts. Mix until well combined.
3. Form dough into sixteen 1" balls. Place in the air fryer basket, working in batches as necessary, and cook 15 minutes until cookies are golden brown and firm. Cool 5 minutes before rolling in confectioners' sugar. Cool completely before serving

PER SERVING (SERVING SIZE: 2 COOKIES)

CALORIES: 410 | **FAT:** 21g | **PROTEIN:** 7g | **SODIUM:** 150mg | **FIBER:** 2g | **CARBOHYDRATES:** 51g | **SUGAR:** 36g

Caramel Baked Apples

This sweet treat is perfect for all ages. If you love caramel apples, you're going to love this dessert. It takes all the best parts from traditional baked apples and adds sweet, gooey goodness to each bite. The apple in this recipe is soft with just a little crunch to keep the texture delicious and fresh without being mushy.

Pantry Staples: granulated sugar
Hands-On Time: 10 minutes
Cook Time: 16 minutes

Serves 4

4 medium Pink Lady apples
½ cup salted butter
8 soft caramel chews
½ cup rolled oats
¼ cup granulated sugar
1 teaspoon ground cinnamon

1. Preheat the air fryer to 350°F.
2. Using a sharp knife, carefully core apples by cutting a large, deep square into the center from the top down. Scoop out seeds and insides, leaving about one-fourth of apple intact at the bottom.
3. In a medium microwave-safe bowl, microwave butter 30 seconds. Add caramels and microwave 15 seconds more. Stir quickly to finish melting caramels into butter.
4. Add oats, sugar, and cinnamon to caramel mixture. Mix until well combined and crumbly.
5. Scoop mixture into cored apples. Place in the air fryer basket and cook 15 minutes until apples are wrinkled and softened. Serve warm.

PER SERVING

CALORIES: 540 | **FAT:** 26g | **PROTEIN:** 3g | **SODIUM:** 260mg | **FIBER:** 5g | **CARBOHYDRATES:** 76g | **SUGAR:** 45g

Chocolate Mayonnaise Cake

If you love fudgy chocolate cakes, you'll love this easy dessert, which uses mayonnaise instead of eggs to give it a super-rich flavor. Don't worry, this cake doesn't taste like mayonnaise. It's so chocolatey and dense, no one will ever suspect your secret ingredient.

Pantry Staples: all-purpose flour, granulated sugar, baking powder, vanilla extract
Hands-On Time: 10 minutes
Cook Time: 25 minutes

Serves 6

1 cup all-purpose flour
½ cup granulated sugar
1 teaspoon baking powder
¼ cup cocoa powder
1 cup mayonnaise
1 teaspoon vanilla extract
½ cup whole milk

1. Preheat the air fryer to 300°F. Spray a 6" round cake pan with cooking spray.
2. In a large bowl, combine flour, sugar, baking powder, and cocoa powder.
3. Stir in mayonnaise, vanilla, and milk. Batter will be thick, but pourable.
4. Pour batter into prepared cake pan. Place in the air fryer basket and cook 25 minutes until a toothpick inserted into the center comes out clean. Serve warm.

PER SERVING

CALORIES: 410 | **FAT:** 29g | **PROTEIN:** 4g | **SODIUM:** 240mg | **FIBER:** 2g | **CARBOHYDRATES:** 36g | **SUGAR:** 18g

Coconut Cupcakes

These cupcakes come together in just 25 minutes, and their light, airy texture lets all the natural flavors shine. Feel free to enjoy them as is or top with coconut whipped cream and a pinch of toasted coconut flakes.

Pantry Staples: all-purpose flour, granulated sugar, baking powder
Hands-On Time: 10 minutes
Cook Time: 15 minutes per batch

Serves 12

1 cup all-purpose flour
½ cup granulated sugar
1 teaspoon baking powder
¼ cup salted butter, melted
1 large egg
½ cup full-fat canned coconut milk
½ cup sweetened shredded coconut

1. Preheat the air fryer to 300°F.
2. In a large bowl, whisk together flour, sugar, and baking powder.
3. Add butter, egg, and coconut milk to dry mixture. Stir until well combined.
4. Fold in shredded coconut. Divide evenly among twelve silicone or aluminum muffin cups, filling each halfway full.
5. Place in the air fryer basket, working in batches as necessary. Cook 15 minutes until brown at the edges and a toothpick inserted into the center comes out clean. Let cool for 5 minutes before serving.

PER SERVING

CALORIES: 150 | **FAT:** 8g | **PROTEIN:** 2g | **SODIUM:** 40mg | **FIBER:** 1g | **CARBOHYDRATES:** 18g | **SUGAR:** 9g

COCONUT WHIPPED CREAM

To make your own coconut whipped cream, place an unopened can of full-fat coconut milk in the refrigerator until chilled (overnight is best). Open and scrape the coconut cream off the top into a bowl. Add ¼ cup confectioners' sugar and 1 teaspoon vanilla extract and whip 2–3 minutes until soft peaks form. This makes a light and flavorful topping in place of frosting.

Lemon Cookies

If you love lemon bars, this cookie will be your new favorite. From the crispy edges to the chewy, tart lemon center, each bite will make you fall more in love.

Pantry Staples: granulated sugar, vanilla extract, all-purpose flour
Hands-On Time: 10 minutes
Cook Time: 42 minutes

Serves 4

- 4 ounces full-fat cream cheese, softened
- ½ cup salted butter, softened
- ⅓ cup granulated sugar
- 1 teaspoon vanilla extract
- 1 cup all-purpose flour
- Zest and juice of 1 medium lemon plus 1 tablespoon lemon juice, divided
- 1 cup confectioners' sugar

1. In a large bowl using a handheld electric mixer, combine cream cheese, butter, granulated sugar, and vanilla. Gradually add flour, lemon zest, and juice of 1 lemon.
2. Chill dough in the refrigerator 30 minutes. While dough is chilling, in a medium bowl, mix confectioners' sugar with remaining 1 tablespoon lemon juice to make a glaze. Set aside.
3. Preheat the air fryer to 300°F. Cut parchment paper to fit the air fryer basket.
4. Form dough into eight 1" balls. Place on parchment paper in the air fryer basket, working in batches as necessary, and cook 12 minutes until edges of the cookies are lightly brown.
5. Spoon glaze over cookies. Cool 10 minutes before serving.

PER SERVING (SERVING SIZE: 2 COOKIES)

CALORIES: 630 | **FAT:** 33g | **PROTEIN:** 5g | **SODIUM:** 270mg | **FIBER:** 1g | **CARBOHYDRATES:** 81g | **SUGAR:** 56g

Cherry Hand Pies

These pies are flaky and deliciously sweet. They're oozing with cherries and buttery flavor. This no-fail dough is perfect for those who aren't familiar with making piecrust. It couldn't be easier to make this tasty dessert.

Pantry Staples: all-purpose flour, granulated sugar
Hands-On Time: 15 minutes
Cook Time: 15 minutes per batch

Serves 6

- **1 cup all-purpose flour**
- **½ cup cold salted butter, grated**
- **5 tablespoons ice water**
- **2 tablespoons granulated sugar**
- **3 cups canned cherry pie filling**
- **1 large egg, whisked**

CHERRY NOT YOUR THING?
Make this recipe using your favorite canned fruit pie filling. Blueberry, peach, and strawberry varieties will all work great.

1. Preheat the air fryer to 320°F. Cut parchment paper to fit the air fryer basket.
2. In a large bowl, mix flour, butter, ice water, and sugar until a soft ball of dough forms.
3. On a lightly floured surface, roll out dough into a 12" × 16" rectangle. Cut dough into six rectangles by cutting across the center, then down into three columns. Each rectangle will be 4" × 8".
4. Place ½ cup pie filling onto the lower half of each rectangle. Fold the top over the filling and press the edges closed with a fork.
5. Using a pastry brush, gently brush top of each pie with egg. Place pies on parchment in the air fryer basket, working in batches as necessary.
6. Cook 15 minutes, turning after 10 minutes, until golden brown and flaky. Let cool 10 minutes before serving.

PER SERVING

CALORIES: 380 | **FAT:** 16g | **PROTEIN:** 4g | **SODIUM:** 160mg | **FIBER:** 1g | **CARBOHYDRATES:** 55g | **SUGAR:** 4g

US/Metric Conversion Chart

VOLUME CONVERSIONS	
US Volume Measure	Metric Equivalent
⅛ teaspoon	0.5 milliliter
¼ teaspoon	1 milliliter
½ teaspoon	2 milliliters
1 teaspoon	5 milliliters
½ tablespoon	7 milliliters
1 tablespoon (3 teaspoons)	15 milliliters
2 tablespoons (1 fluid ounce)	30 milliliters
¼ cup (4 tablespoons)	60 milliliters
⅓ cup	90 milliliters
½ cup (4 fluid ounces)	125 milliliters
⅔ cup	160 milliliters
¾ cup (6 fluid ounces)	180 milliliters
1 cup (16 tablespoons)	250 milliliters
1 pint (2 cups)	500 milliliters
1 quart (4 cups)	1 liter (about)

WEIGHT CONVERSIONS	
US Weight Measure	Metric Equivalent
½ ounce	15 grams
1 ounce	30 grams
2 ounces	60 grams
3 ounces	85 grams
¼ pound (4 ounces)	115 grams
½ pound (8 ounces)	225 grams
¾ pound (12 ounces)	340 grams
1 pound (16 ounces)	454 grams

OVEN TEMPERATURE CONVERSIONS	
Degrees Fahrenheit	Degrees Celsius
200 degrees F	95 degrees C
250 degrees F	120 degrees C
275 degrees F	135 degrees C
300 degrees F	150 degrees C
325 degrees F	160 degrees C
350 degrees F	180 degrees C
375 degrees F	190 degrees C
400 degrees F	205 degrees C
425 degrees F	220 degrees C
450 degrees F	230 degrees C

BAKING PAN SIZES	
American	Metric
8 x 1½ inch round baking pan	20 x 4 cm cake tin
9 x 1½ inch round baking pan	23 x 3.5 cm cake tin
11 x 7 x 1½ inch baking pan	28 x 18 x 4 cm baking tin
13 x 9 x 2 inch baking pan	30 x 20 x 5 cm baking tin
2 quart rectangular baking dish	30 x 20 x 3 cm baking tin
15 x 10 x 2 inch baking pan	30 x 25 x 2 cm baking tin (Swiss roll tin)
9 inch pie plate	22 x 4 or 23 x 4 cm pie plate
7 or 8 inch springform pan	18 or 20 cm springform or loose bottom cake tin
9 x 5 x 3 inch loaf pan	23 x 13 x 7 cm or 2 lb narrow loaf or pâté tin
1½ quart casserole	1.5 liter casserole
2 quart casserole	2 liter casserole

Index